Myths in Education

Myths in Education

*Beliefs That Hinder Progress
and Their Alternatives*

ARTHUR W. COMBS
University of Northern Colorado

ALLYN AND BACON, INC.   *Boston, London, Sydney*

Interior cartoons by Ric Estrada / Superscript Associates

Production Editor: Nancy Doherty
Series Editor: Steven Mathews

Library of Congress Cataloging in Publication Data

Combs, Arthur Wright.
  Myths in education.

  Bibliography: p.
  1. Combs, Arthur Wright. 2. Education—Philosophy.
3. Education—Aims and objectives. I. Title.
LA885.C65   370.1   78-17338
ISBN 0-205-06021-8
ISBN 0-205-05984-4 pbk.

Printed in the United States of America.

Contents

v

Preface

For more than thirty years I have served as a consultant to schools and colleges in every state in the United States. Out of that experience, I have concluded that the myths we firmly believe are the greatest current source of failure in our public schools. They are also the greatest deterrent to innovation and change. Myths are false or inaccurate beliefs that are generally held to be true. Since people behave in terms of their beliefs, action based on false or inaccurate assumptions can only result in false or inaccurate outcomes, the hindrance of progress, contribution to the status quo, frustrated school personnel, and great damage to students—the very people schools are designed to assist.

The insidious thing about myths is people believe they are true. People never doubt their assumptions and so they cannot account for errors or failure to achieve hoped for results. Myths have hampered progress and frustrated the achievement of human goals throughout history. They are still at it. In education they exist by the dozens. If today's schools are to meet the challenges of our changing society, we must break ourselves loose from the myths that bind us.

An educational consultant is in a position something like that of the old-time minstrel. Minstrels went from place to place listening, observing, and building the news into songs to be sung in still other towns and villages. The songs were continually changing to include new information the minstrel picked up as he traveled and to suit the needs and conditions of the audience. Some songs had very short lives as the events they described faded from public interest. Others became permanent parts of the minstrel's repertoire, adapted and refined from new observations and tested on countless critical audiences. A minstrel's very best songs were a kind of extract, drawn from much experience, distilled in his mind and delivered in the minstrel's personal style. Consultants are like that. They have rich opportunities to observe and participate in the problem-solving efforts of teachers and administrators in a wide variety of settings. In the process, their own beliefs are refined about students, teachers, administrators, and the thinking and practices required for effective learning and schools. This book contains some of my songs about myths and the damage they do to students and schools.

I am deeply grateful to the thousands of parents, teachers, counselors, and administrators with whom I have worked at every level of public and private education. Together we have wrestled with the problems of understanding youth, of revising and improving instruction, and of finding better ways to meet the educational needs of a changing world. Time after time in this process, we found our way blocked by myths about people, learning, motivation, and ways of dealing with students and school personnel. As a consequence, over a period of ten to fifteen years, I catalogued the myths we confronted and explored their dynamics with dozens of working groups. The response by these groups of school people to the exploration of myths was so unfailingly positive and enthusiastic, and the exploration so helpful for my own professional life, I have written this book about myths in the hope it may prove useful to an even wider audience.

A.W.C.

Introduction:
Myths That Bind Us

People behave according to their beliefs. If I believe a man is honest, I'll trust him. If I don't believe he's honest, I won't. Each of us behaves in terms of what we feel is so. When human beliefs are accurate and positive, great progress can often be made in human affairs; when they are false or negative, progress is hampered, hopes and desires are frustrated, and human life itself may be jeopardized.

Every generation has been the victim of its own myths. When people believed that illness was a function of bad blood, it seemed completely rational to cure disease by draining the bad blood. People were bled when they got sick and, sometimes, they were bled to death. When people believed that the world was flat, they avoided what they perceived to be the edge so they wouldn't fall off. When they believed that the mentally ill were possessed by the devil, treatment was designed to drive the devil out. When people believed that children were small-sized adults, child labor was regarded as acceptable and play was regarded as something to be gotten over with as quickly as possible. Myths like these have done incalculable harm to human beings through the ages. They still do. Today we are just as much the victims of our own myths as our ancestors were the victims of theirs.

THE NATURE OF MYTHS

A *myth* is a widely held belief that is not true. But people behave in terms of their beliefs and the damage done to human thought and action by the myths people hold is incalculable. Myths are major factors behind inefficiency of institutions, breakdowns in communication, and failures to cope with many modern problems. In educational thinking and practice, they create a continuous barrier to innovation and change.

Five characteristics of myths cause them to be especially treacherous in human affairs:

1. They are generally held.
2. They are often expressed as dichotomies.
3. They sometimes contain a germ of truth.
4. They justify behavior.
5. They often become institutionalized.

Myths Are Generally Held

That myths are so widely believed protects them from careful scrutiny. They tend to corroborate themselves because no one stops to question them. They seem self-evident and are often preceded by such comments as: "It is clear that . . . ," "As everyone knows . . . ," or "It's true. . . ." And of course there's little point in questioning matters that "everyone knows are true." Besides, raising questions about well-established ideas can make one an object of ridicule or incur the wrath of "right thinking" people. Myths may continue for generations simply because they're never seriously challenged. This results in what Charles Silberman, a noted educational critic, calls *mindlessness*, a state in which people do things simply because "it has always been so." [1]

Myths Are Often Expressed as Dichotomies

Sometimes explicitly, sometimes by suggestion or innuendo, people everywhere state important issues in either-or terms. It is much simpler to categorize people and events as black or white, Republican or Democratic, American or Communist. Dichotomies have the precious characteristic of definiteness. They make things neat and tidy. Unfortunately, it is possible to become so accustomed to thinking in dichotomies that we begin to delude ourselves that there are no other choices. We categorize children as naughty or nice, bosses as for us or against us, women as beautiful or homely. We can go out or stay home, like someone or dislike him or her. In reacting to other people, we can cooperate or compete, attack or appease. When used to describe situations to which they do not apply, dichotomies can be extremely dangerous. Earl Kelley, author and keen observer of modern education, once said to me, "Whenever you find an idea that can be expressed as either-or, it is almost certain they are both wrong." Myths are often like that.

Myths Sometimes Contain a Germ of Truth

An even more insidious source of sabotage from myths lies in the fact that sometimes they are partially based on truth. Our ancestors, for example, believed that disease was a function of bad blood; today we know that some diseases are, indeed, accompanied by disturbances of blood chemistry. Similarly, our forefathers' fear that night air caused illness probably had some basis in fact; mosquitoes flew at night and frequently carried malaria and yellow fever germs. Such elements of truth, unhappily, have the effect of corroborating myths and encourage continued thinking in the same directions. Donald Snygg said: "There is nothing in this world more dangerous than a partly right idea. Because they sometimes result in partly right solutions we are encouraged to continue our explorations in the same directions. Sometimes you can sell more papers by shouting louder on the same corner. But, sometimes, you need to find another corner." [2] The problem with myths is similar. The small elements of truth they sometimes contain encourage us to try a little harder, a little longer, a little more precisely on the same assumptions. And so they keep us forever locked into partial solutions when we might better be searching for more accurate understandings.

Even the most fantastic notions for dealing with people, sometimes, under some circumstances, get results. Psychologists know that almost anything will result in a change in human behavior, especially if the subject "believes" it will help. One needs but review some of the fads for human improvement that have swept the country over the last twenty years, such as weird diets, bizarre religious groups, and shoddy gurus or demagogues of a dozen varieties, to see recurring examples of this principle in action.

Myths Justify Behavior

A fourth reason why myths have such malignant effects is they frequently support our preferred behavior. They affirm and endorse the things we would rather do anyhow. The southern slaveholder could justify his ownership of human beings by the myth that slaves were chattels, not people. He could even live with pride in himself and in the eyes of his fellows, seeing himself as a man of great compassion taking care of creatures who could not take care of themselves. People are notorious for finding good reasons for the things they would rather do. In times of war, whole nations can be caught up in the myth that "God is on our side."

Myths can also justify a lack of behavior when that is more comfortable or desirable. Modern citizens can justify their failures to deal with the problem of slums with: "Those people like it that way. Give them a house and they'll make it a pig sty." It is much easier and more comfortable to live with what seems to be working than to raise questions which might require change or force us to look at ourselves in less favorable lights.

Myths Often Become Institutionalized

Some myths in almost every society are provided a kind of sanctity by custom or conscious design. Either way, they become exempt from examination or question. Some, like the myth of competition we will examine later, evolve in a particular culture over long periods, probably as an outgrowth of that culture's peculiar struggles to solve its problems. Others, like some dietary restrictions established in the early churches, were probably consciously designed by priests as a means to protect their people from illness. A myth, stated as a revelation from God, is an extraordinarily difficult thing to change. Persons living under the myth are not even permitted the luxury of questioning it, for questioning, itself, may be regarded as sinful.

The use of myths by people in power is not confined to religion or times past. Myths have been employed by despots and demagogues for political control down to the present. Hitler's myth of the "pure Aryan and unclean Jew" was a powerful means of controlling the German people. More recently, politicians have used myths of ethnic differences to promote their candidacy for office, from local school board elections to campaigns for the highest offices in the land.

MYTHS IN EDUCATION

Whatever the sources of myths and whatever the reasons for their continued existence, the destructive effects they wield upon our society are immense. When basic assumptions are inaccurate, everything predicated upon those assumptions is in error too, and negative outcomes are multiplied over and over. This is bad enough in ordinary times. But when the pressure of changing times demands that institutions drastically overhaul themselves, the existence of myths is especially disastrous; they interfere with the search for viable alternatives. Innovations designed to meet new demands, for example, may begin with the same old faulty assumptions and end by doing little more than polishing and repolishing what was already not good enough.

Currently, our system of education in the United States is being castigated for its failure to adapt to modern needs. There is disappointment nationwide with the outcomes of education and increasing demands for "accountability"—insistence that schools and teachers clearly demonstrate that money poured into the system is getting real results.[3] Much of what goes on in our schools is increasingly regarded as irrelevant by the public, teachers, and students alike. In response, massive efforts are being mounted by state and federal agencies to encourage innovations. Huge amounts of financial and human resources are being poured into the effort to make schools more adequate. A vast ferment is occurring with hundreds of solutions being loudly proclaimed by their inventors or practitioners. Out of such ferment good things can happen; important innovations may spring into being. But much of this effort is doomed to failure because the basic myths which got education into trouble in the first place have not been questioned.

Education's present troubles are not going to be resolved by a tinkering job. The need for change is too great. What is required is a reexamination of fundamental assumptions and the creation of curricula and practices more relevant to the needs of modern youth and modern society. This will not be easy; over the years our educational system has acquired an extraordinary number of beliefs and practices that stand as roadblocks to the achievement of modern goals. Some of these are administrative, some are curricular, some are time-honored customs, traditions, and methods employed by classroom teachers.

Examination of almost any school will reveal an incredible number of barriers that were established at some time in the past for good reason, but exist today with no discernible justification beyond tradition. Many of these barriers came into being as expressions of myths widespread in our society. Others have roots in inaccurate concepts about the nature of human beings, in myths about child growth and development, or in long-outmoded concepts about learning. Whatever their origin, if we are to meet the challenge of modern times, a first step must be to eliminate dozens of myths that have blocked and distorted our thinking for generations. We need to bring these myths to light, and replace them with principles based on up-to-date information about people and their behavior.

The first place from which myths must be eliminated is from within educators, themselves. A mature and responsible teaching profession cannot be grounded in mythology. What distinguishes a profession from more mechanical occupations is the operation of the professional worker as a thinking, problem-solving human being. Whatever educators do must be for some good and sufficient reason, defensible in terms more rational than custom, tradition, or convenience. There is no place for mythology in a profession.

Research on the helping professions carried out at the University of Florida[4] and elsewhere[5] demonstrates that effective "helpers" can be clearly distinguished from ineffective ones on the basis of their belief systems. These studies suggest that "good" practitioners have clear, accurate, and consistent beliefs about themselves, about the nature of those they work with, and about their own purposes and those of society in carrying out their tasks. To achieve such characteristics requires a continuous process of exploring and discovering a highly personal, congruent, and meaningful set of beliefs. An important part of that process must be the weeding of myths from the professional worker's thinking, practice, and procedures. This book is designed to begin that exploration.

THE PURPOSE OF THIS BOOK

For the remainder of this book I intend to explore some of the more common myths that bind those of us in education and to suggest more promising alternatives. For convenience I have organized the myths into three groups:

1. **Cultural Myths.** These are widespread misconceptions in our society. Such myths have inevitable effects on our educational system.

2. **Myths About Persons and Behavior.** These concern what people believe about the nature of human beings and their potentials. We will especially consider myths about children and their relationships to the world they live in.

3. **Myths About Learning and Schooling.** These are inaccurate concepts about teaching, motivating, evaluating, and working with students in the classroom.

In addition to exploring and exposing educational myths, a number of related readings are listed at the end of each chapter. These are for the benefit of readers who would like to think more deeply about these matters.

Merely calling attention to myths is not enough. What is needed are clearer, more accurate concepts on which to predicate action. I have, therefore, tried not only to shed some light on false and partially true aspects of myths, but to state more accurate, supportable bases for action.

Some of the myths I have included may seem obvious to you; others may start you thinking in new directions. It may even come as a surprise to find some of your own beliefs included as myths. These are probably the ones you need to examine most carefully. I expect you'll agree with some of my conclusions; others you may find doubtful, even distasteful. No matter. The important thing is not whether I am right or wrong, but your own experiences in clarifying your personal systems of belief. If the examination of myths provided by this book initiates that, we will both have reason to rest content.

NOTES

1. C. E. Silberman, *Crisis in the Classroom* (New York: Random House, Inc., 1970), p. 2.
2. D. Snygg and A. W. Combs, *Individual Behavior: A New Frame of Reference for Psychology* (New York: Harper and Brothers, 1949), p. 4.
3. A. W. Combs, *Educational Accountability: Beyond Behavioral Objectives* (Washington, D.C.: Association for Supervision and Curriculum Development, 1972), p. 7.
4. *See* the following:

Robert G. Brown, "A Study of the Perceptual Organization of Elementary and Secondary Outstanding Young Educators" (unpublished doctoral dissertation, University of Florida, 1970);

A. W. Combs, *Florida Studies in the Helping Professions*, Social Science Monograph No. 37 (Gainesville, Fl.: University of Florida Press, 1969);

Charles Van Loan Dedrick, "The Relationship Between Perceptual Characteristics and Effective Teaching at the Junior College Level" (unpublished doctoral dissertation, University of Florida, 1972);

Donald A. Dellow, "A Study of the Perceptual Organization of Teachers and Conditions of Empathy, Congruence, and Positive Regard" (unpublished doctoral dissertation, University of Florida, 1971);

Gerald Douglas Jennings, "The Relationship Between Perceptual Characteristics and Effective Advising of University Housing Para-Professional Residence Assistants" (unpublished doctoral dissertation, University of Florida, 1973);

Anne O'Roark, "A Comparison of Perceptual Characteristics of Elected Legislators and Public School Counselors Identified as Most and Least Effective" (unpublished doctoral dissertation, University of Florida, 1975);

Herman G. Vonk, "The Relationship of Teacher Effectiveness to Perception of Self and Teaching Purposes" (unpublished doctoral dissertation, University of Florida, 1970).

5. *See also* the following:

Chunghoon Choy, "The Relationship of College Teacher Effectiveness to Conceptual Systems Orientation and Perceptual

Orientation" (unpublished doctoral dissertation, University of Northern Colorado, 1969);

Eunice J. Doyle, "The Relationship Between College Teacher Effectiveness and Inferred Characteristics of the Adequate Personality" (unpublished doctoral dissertation, University of Northern Colorado, 1969);

B. Koffman, "A Comparison of the Perceptual Organizations of Outstanding and Randomly Selected Teachers in 'Open' and 'Traditional' Classrooms" (unpublished doctoral dissertation, University of Massachusetts, 1975).

Robert E. Morgenstern, "The Relationship Between Two Modes of Interpersonal Conditions and College Teacher Effectiveness" (unpublished doctoral dissertation, University of Northern Colorado, 1969);

Lois P. Picht, "Self-Concept in Relation to Effectiveness in Student Teaching" (unpublished doctoral dissertation, University of Northern Colorado, 1969);

Richard Usher and John Hanke, "Third Force in Psychology and College Teacher Effectiveness Research at the University of Northern Colorado," *Colorado Journal of Educational Research* 10 (Winter 1971): p. 2;

PART I

MYTHS FROM AMERICAN CULTURE

Many of the myths affecting public schools in the United States are cultural—deeply rooted in custom and tradition—and so have inevitable effects on all of our society's institutions, including the public schools. Such myths are so much a part of the world we grow up in that they are automatically accepted without question. They are part of the reality we experience and have pervading effects on every aspect of the institutions we build and the lives we live. They are also most difficult to change.

Cultural myths are occasionally questioned by some hardy souls. Such actions are likely to threaten the culture and are usually met with some kind of defensive reaction. Persons who deviate and question the established myths may at first be simply ignored. If the issues are pressed so they cannot be ignored, then doubters may be ridiculed, isolated, or shunned by all "right thinking" people. If the questioning becomes too pressing, the society may feel so threatened that it reacts by attempting to imprison or annihilate offenders. People do not take kindly to efforts to change long-standing myths.

Because of their pervasive character, cultural myths greatly affect education and seriously interfere with the processes of change and adaptation to the needs of new generations. Precisely because they are so generally held, it is even more necessary to explore them so they can be openly confronted and subjected to careful analysis.

This part examines a few of the cultural myths that exert profound effects on our educational system. Even though we're aware of these myths, we probably cannot change their acceptance in society at large. As educators, however, we can help prevent their destructive effects on the schools and the students we work with. By clarifying our own understandings we may become more clearly aware of the roadblocks cultural myths pose for innovation and change. That, in turn, may free us to find more adequate bases for thinking about goals and practices for meeting the changing demands of our times.

The Myth of
Our Competitive Society

"Schools should prepare young people to live in our competitive society." To millions in the United States that principle seems self-evident. It is also endorsed, more's the pity, by thousands of teachers and school administrators. The statement, in fact, is almost totally false; the damage done in its name, however, is colossal. A school system that glorifies competition will, almost certainly, fail to prepare its students to live effectively in the modern world. The notion that ours is primarily a competitive society is a myth. Actually, we live in the most cooperative, interdependent society the world has ever known.[1]

OUR COOPERATIVE SOCIETY

Two great trends in human history have made cooperation an absolute must for our contemporary way of life: (1) the ever increasing dependence of people on one another, and (2) the tremendous increase of power in the hands of individuals.

The world has become a very small place, where we live, almost literally, in each other's laps. We are dependent on people we have never seen or heard of to produce and deliver our food, clothing, shelter and safety. So simple a thing as a

15

quart of milk would never reach us without the smooth cooperation of thousands of unknown friends who produce, process,
and transport it from the cow to our local store. Thousands
more produce the machinery for raising cow feed, for pasteur-
izing and bottling the milk, and for building the roads and
vehicles that make its transportation possible.

We may be impressed by the competitive features of our
society and we may like to think of ourselves as essentially a
competitive people, but the net effect of the many industrial
and scientific advances of the last one hundred years has been
to make us all thoroughly dependent upon millions of other
people. From the engineers who keep the electric turbines running through the night to the garbage collectors who keep our
cities livable, each of us must rely on others to carry out tasks
we cannot perform ourselves. Few of us could live for more
than a very short time apart from others. Whether we like it
or not, we are thoroughly and completely dependent upon the
goodwill and cooperation of others at every moment of our
lives. In turn, thousands of other people are dependent on us.
We are indeed "our brothers' keepers" as never before in history.

Not only has our dependence on others increased in the
past hundred years, but the power a single individual can exert on others in the society has increased as well. Anyone can
purchase instruments for life or death at any hardware or drug
store. One untrustworthy person running amok with a rifle
can throw our whole society into chaos by shooting a president
or a Martin Luther King. Even the least of us has power of
life or death over others. Each of us has large amounts of
electrical power at our fingertips in the nearest light switch.
Behind the wheels of our cars we are capable of dealing death
and destruction on city streets or highways. Such individual
power necessitates cooperation for our society to run smoothly.
We could not even go to the supermarket if we could not trust
other individuals not to harm us along the way. We could not
drive at all unless we could count on others to cooperate by

staying on their side of the road. Imagine driving in a truly competitive society!

Even our large industries, to which we point with pride as samples of our competitive way of life, turn out, on closer analysis, to be outstanding examples of cooperation. Although they loudly proclaim the virtues of competition, large industrial organizations are thoroughly dependent upon the smooth integration of thousands of interdependent workers. We forget that one of the great contributions to modern industry was the development by Henry Ford of the assembly line—a highly organized method of getting people to cooperate in the manufacture of a product. Our large "competitive" industries are actually marvels of cooperative effort and, further, they do not really want to compete. It has even been necessary for Congress to pass stringent antitrust laws to prevent them from eliminating competition altogether.

It's true that sometimes we compete with others in our society, but competition is not the rule; it is the exception. We need only reflect on our own lives in the past twenty-four hours to discover how overwhelmingly cooperative, and how seldom competitive, our behavior has been. We live for days without competing with others; we cooperate from morning to night. What a strange twist that in the face of these facts, we continue to describe our society, not in terms of what we do most, but in terms of what we do only seldomly.

WHO COMPETES?

Why is it then, that in the face of all this contradictory evidence, we continue to think of ourselves as a competitive people? One reason seems to be perspective. There are, indeed, some special places in which competition is useful or enjoyable. We tend to generalize from those special occasions to the belief that competition is the "American way." For example, we often employ competition to deal with scarcity. When there are fewer places in colleges than students applying for admission, students are forced to compete to get in. When there is not enough food, clothing, housing, money, or even tickets to the World Series, we resort to competition to decide who gets them.

Competition is also used in the determination of quality. A way of choosing between two candidates for office, for example, is to have them compete in the public eye. We do the same thing when we compare two or more products of nearly equal quality to determine which is better.

Another reason why we glorify competition probably arises from the excitement competing engenders in sporting events and from our own personal experiences of exhilaration when playing a game against a worthy opponent. Such feelings are deeply satisfying and stimulating. It is not surprising that such good feelings should be translated into the belief that competition is a good and desirable aspect of life. Of course it is. As a game, or as a way of handling scarcity, or as a means to choose between political candidates, competition can be useful. But as a universal way of life it leaves much to be desired; and as a goal for education it is a disaster. To teach our children, who must live in a cooperative world, that competition is the way to be a success in life is teaching them to live in a world that does not exist. Fortunately, children vigorously resist such instruction. We are lucky indeed that they never quite fall for the deception. Instead, they quickly learn for themselves the value of working together and cooperate with one another just like the grownups they see around them.

SOME EFFECTS OF COMPETITION

Any practice we use to achieve our goals must be examined in light of its side effects both on the practitioner and on others. When examined, competition can be found to have several adverse effects on people. One such effect is to make the people who are competing more alike. Competition can only work if people agree to seek the same goals and follow the same rules. Accordingly, as competitors strive to beat each other's records, they tend to become more alike. If total conformity is what we want in our society, worshiping competition is one effective way to get it. Price tags on our practices must be read not only in terms of visible, concrete outcomes, but also in terms of the less visible, human consequences that may in the long run be far more important.

Advocating competition as a way of life also produces a concomitant belief that, of necessity, someone must win and someone must lose in life's activities. Few of us would be willing to accept such a dog-eat-dog concept as a basic guideline for living together in our democratic, cooperative society. Applied to the education of children, this principle instigates a myriad of problems. The primary goal of our public schools must be the optimal development of every child. Practices which seriously interfere with that goal must surely be examined with great care.

George Leonard, author and educational critic, cites another effect—that competition for its own sake leads only to emptiness.

> There is nothing wrong with competition in the proper proportion. Like a little salt, it adds zest to the game and to life itself.
>
> But when the seasoning is mistaken for the substance, only sickness can follow. Similarly, when winning becomes "the only thing" it can lead only to eventual emptiness and anomie.[2]

Competition also tends to destroy feelings of trust in ourselves and others. The kind of interdependent, cooperative society we live in necessitates that people be able to depend on one another. But, by glorifying winning at the cost of human values, competition produces fear of other people. This is in direct contradiction to the kind of attitude required for a successful cooperative society. A person cannot cooperate effectively with people he or she fears.

The success of a society based on democratic principles, such as ours, depends on the production of independent people of dignity who can be counted on to operate in ways likely to be fulfilling both to themselves and to their fellow citizens. What undermines respect for one's self or others is dangerous for all of us. Whether we like it or not, we are completely dependent on the goodwill of our fellows at every moment of our modern complex existence. What destroys trust in ourselves or others makes communication difficult and cripples cooperative effort.

Public schools are charged with the responsibility of preparing youth to become effective citizens. To meet that expectation, schools cannot afford to predicate goals and practices on false assumptions about the world they are readying students to enter. Preparing students to live and work in a complex, cooperative society requires, at the very least, such goals as the following: autonomy, responsibility, willingness to pull one's fair share of the load, concern and tolerance for others, appreciation of human values, commitment to human welfare, commitment to democratic principles, respect for the dignity and integrity of every human being, and the necessary skills and understandings to participate effectively in personal and group interaction. Such objectives do not preclude the achievement of excellence in traditional content and subject matter. They determine how such excellence will be put to use in the broader society in which students must spend the rest of their lives.

NOTES

1. Much of the material in this chapter has been adapted from an article by the author: "The Myth of Competition" by Arthur W. Combs. From *Childhood Education*, February 1957, Vol-

ume 33, Number 6, pp. 264–269. Adapted by permission of the Association for Childhood Education International, 3615 Wisconsin Avenue, N.W., Washington, D.C. 20016.
2. As quoted by Donald Kaul, "Over the Coffee: On Winning and Learning," Des Moines *Register*, October 4, 1973, p. 20.

SELECTED READINGS

Brocedy, H. S. "Comprehensive High School as an Instrument of the Culture." *North Central Association Quarterly* 50 (1975): 295–98.

Green, T. F. *Work, Leisure and the American Schools.* New York: Random House, Inc., 1968.

Marrow, A. J. *Management by Participation: Creating a Climate for Personal and Organizational Development.* New York: Harper & Row, Publishers, 1967.

Roethlisberger, F. J. *Man in Organization.* Cambridge, Mass.: Harvard University Press, 1968.

Webb, R. B. "Youth Life-Worlds and the American Culture." *Feeling, Valuing and the Art of Growing* (1977 Yearbook). Washington, D.C.: Association for Supervision and Curriculum Development, 1977.

Worth Commission on Educational Planning. *A Future of Choices: A Choice of Futures.* Edmonton, Canada: Huntig, 1972.

Myths About Democracy

Three myths about democracy that are common to our culture create serious barriers to the processes of education. They are:

1. Democracy means treating everyone alike.
2. Democracy is rule by the majority.
3. Democracy is taking a vote.

TREATING EVERYONE ALIKE

For many people, democracy means treating everyone the same way. This myth seems to arise out of the egalitarian principle that "all men are created equal," a noble principle indeed. Having a universal reverence for life, however, does not demand that all persons be treated exactly alike. As a matter of fact, few of us would *really* want everyone to be treated alike. That could make life very uncomfortable. Whether we would, or would not, like to see everyone treated the same way is also influenced by our economic condition— whether we are "haves" or "have nots." To a "have not," identically equal treatment seems desirable and right; to a "have," it is usually regarded as unfair and a violation of personal rights. Like most myths, this one is usually employed to justify what is comfortable and convenient.

Human beings are infinitely unique. No two have ever been, or ever will be, completely alike. In the face of this infinite uniqueness, equal treatment of all would result in the grossest kinds of injustice and in a society totally insensitive to the needs of its citizens. What is needed, then, is not that all members of society be treated alike, but that each be treated in the light of his or her individual needs. Public schools, above all, must be predicated upon that basic principle. Unhappily, the myth of equal treatment, that is so widespread in our society, has its inevitable expression in our public schools. Its application there produces unbelievable problems, usually in the holy name of fairness.

Human uniqueness has long been acknowledged, but our schools continue to search for ways of treating people alike, with the myth that that is the "democratic way" giving comfort and solace to those who wish to maintain the status quo. For at least one hundred years, educators have known that meeting the needs of individual children requires personalizing instruction—fitting the curriculum to the needs of the student. Nevertheless, we persist in seeking ways to fit students to the curriculum and use the equal treatment myth to justify such action. Schools are organized, rules are made, and methods are constructed to assure that all children will be treated alike. More often than not, this leads to the protection of time-honored practices when updating is called for, support of purely administrative expedients, and the general persistence of the status quo.

Even young children are keenly aware of how unfair it is to treat everyone alike. I once asked a bright little girl how she felt about the fact that her teacher gave more attention to the poor readers in her class. "Oh, that's all right," she said, "they need it." Children know and understand that fairness does not require equal treatment, but, rather, attention to individual need. They are not likely to be distressed by a child getting what he or she needs; what angers them is a particular child getting much more than needed. Teachers' pets have always been anathema to their classmates. It is a pity that the natural acceptance of human uniqueness so well understood in childhood is so badly distorted in adulthood. We cannot afford to allow the myth of equal treatment to continue to block our thinking about educational reform. The cost is too great in missed opportunities and waste of precious human resources.

MAJORITY RULE BY TAKING A VOTE

Two other myths about democracy assert that democracy requires rule by the majority, and the way to achieve that rule is by taking a vote. Calling for a vote, however, often actually serves to undermine the democratic process by being no more than a means of stopping discussion, an administrative technique designed to get on with whatever business is at hand. A vote can also be little more than an acceptable form of coercion. It is usually called for when someone in the group believes that enough people have been swayed to his way of thinking to commit the group to his mode of action. Once taken, the vote is then perceived by the majority as a warrant to get on with whatever the decision entails. For those in the minority, the vote may be seen quite differently as an act of oppression and coercion. "A man convinced against his will is of the same opinion still," the saying goes. The defeated party, far from agreeing with the verdict, may come to the conclusion that he or she has "been had." Such a feeling, in turn, may contribute to the conclusion that he or she is not really bound by the vote at all.

The goal of school must be to aid each student to achieve maximum potential. That is an individual matter; it is not de-

cided by taking a vote. Making decisions solely on the basis
of majority rule is to confuse a form occasionally useful for
making group decisions with the fundamental democratic belief in the dignity and integrity of individuals.

THE FORM AND THE ESSENCE

Myths about democracy, like those we have been discussing,
are a consequence of confusing the form for the essence, a
common error in human thinking. Throughout history, the
pursuit of magnificent ideas has been subverted or prostituted
by preoccupation with the methods, procedures, or ceremonies
meant to express those ideas. The teachings of Christ have
sometimes been demeaned by forms of the church; lofty concepts about human freedom have been desecrated by the very
political structures designed to insure them. The essence of
democracy lies, not in its forms, but in its fundamental belief
that "when people are free they can find their own best ways."
Such a tenet is not a technique or practice; it is a fundamental
statement about the nature of human beings, about human
potentialities and what is needed to fulfill them; it says more
about the need for protection of minorities than rule by the
majority.

The democratic principle, to be sure, has important implications for the ways people deal with one another. But the
forms, institutions, practices, or procedures devised to imple-
ment the belief are no more than expressions by which it is
hoped the belief may be fulfilled. A basic belief in democracy
does not demand that everyone decide. Quite the contrary.
It calls for faith in our fellows, so that many times we will be
content to let them decide for us. In a complex society everyone cannot be expertly informed on all matters. We are forced
to rely upon the intelligence and goodwill of those who are
informed to make decisions for us. The more complex the so-

ciety, the more such faith must be employed. Our representative form of government is an expression of that principle. Our public schools should be another.

One would think that schools, charged with the cultivation of youth, would be our most outstanding models of democracy in action. Alas, this is far from the truth. Even the most cursory examination of schools at every level will reveal a bewildering array of practices and procedures far out of touch with basic democratic concepts. Often these practices are shrugged off with the remark that "these are only kids," as though democratic values did not apply to youth. It took an action of the U.S. Supreme Court to affirm that students had rights like any other citizen. Many teachers and administrators still find that principle hard to accept. Inhibiting, destructive influences are even proclaimed in some schools as evidence of quality instruction or are proudly justified by one of the myths about democracy. Children learn much more from what they experience than from what they are formally taught. If schools are to truly express the democratic belief, they cannot afford to substitute forms for the essence or to predicate goals, practices, and procedures on myths.

Democratic principles *can* work and *do* work as hundreds of fine teachers in American schools have demonstrated. This is not to say that running schools democratically is either simple or easy. Democratic ways of living must be learned by teachers and students alike and that learning takes time, opportunity, and motivation. Democratic principles will work in schools if they are clearly understood and truly valued by staff and administration. Trying to teach children to "do what I say—not what I do" has never been a fruitful approach to education. The best preparation for life in a democratic society is being brought up in one. Schools are society's institutions and ought to mirror the best society stands for. To do this calls for clear discrimination between form and essence, principle and myth.

SELECTED READINGS

Association for Supervision and Curriculum Development. *Life Skills in School and Society* (1969 Yearbook). Washington, D.C.: Association for Supervision and Curriculum Development, 1969.

Educational Leadership. Entire May 31, 1974 issue on student rights.

Farson, R. "Forum: Birthrights—A Children's Bill of Rights." *Ms* 11 (1974): 66–70.

Fromm, E. *The Sane Society.* New York: Holt, Rinehart and Winston, 1953.

Kohlberg, L. "Cognitive Developmental Approach to Moral Education." *Phi Delta Kappan* 56 (1975): 670–77.

Sanchez, R. *Schooling American Society: A Democratic Ideology.* Syracuse, N.Y.: Syracuse University Press, 1976.

The Credentials Myth

The credentials myth maintains that holding special credentials insures the possessor greater wisdom or dependability. It might equally be called the specialist myth or the expert myth. Whatever its name, it refers to the belief that persons with special titles, licenses, or positions are somehow endowed with greater credibility than the rest of us; whatever a person with a title (president, mayor, teacher, doctor, commentator, editor, father, mother) says must surely be better. Sometimes this is true, but probably far less often than most people assume.

Credentialing of professions is society's way of assuring at least a minimum of confidence in persons claiming special skill in one field or another. Professions seeking such credentials always do so with the claim that they are necessary to protect the public from quackery. Once established "for the protection of the public," credentials often become little more than means of establishing job security; they limit the number of persons who can enter the profession while they increase the prestige and income of the licensees. Thus, doctors, lawyers, midwives, psychologists, barbers, accountants, beauticians, teachers, administrators, and many others seek legislation establishing their profession as a kind of closed shop.

This restraint of trade has become so widespread that a number of legislatures are reexamining the desirability of professional licenses.

THE ARROGANCE OF POSITION

The specialist-is-better myth has many expressions in our educational system. In the classroom, it leads to an expectation that the teacher knows and the student does not. This fountainhead of knowledge syndrome places terrible pressures on teachers who must work under the necessity of always being right, a demand few teachers can ever hope to meet. Teachers who permit themselves to be seduced into such roles are almost certain to lead unhappy lives in our increasingly complex society. The ever-widening generation gaps make it further unlikely that information important to the teacher will also be important to students.

If students are also seduced into believing the credentials myth, the outcome is equally negative. Reliance on teacher authority destroys initiative, cuts off questioning, and results in dull and apathetic approaches to learning. The very heart of creativity is questioning. Anything that gets in the way of the student's questioning is likely to be destructive of one of the major goals of the educational process. In the long run, reliance on the specialty myth is quite likely to result in ever-widening gulfs between teachers and students.

The credentials myth is generally accompanied by conscious attempts on the part of the specialist to glorify his or her position. Being an expert is a heady business and the temptation to embellish the prestige and status of the credential is almost irresistible. Often this goes so far that experts begin to believe they are indeed infallible and they create various put-downs for those who encroach, no matter how slightly, on the hallowed ground of their specialty. This can destroy people's confidence in their capacities to deal with the problems they confront. A good example is to be seen in what has happened to educational research in the last generation. Twenty-five years ago "action research" in education was widely advocated. Action research held that all teachers had research responsibilities and ought to be involved in one way or another with research activities in their own schools and in their own classrooms. This promising movement is now practically dead. We have turned research over to the "experts" holding doctoral degrees in statistics and research. With fantastic arrogance these experts have preempted educational research and intimidated teachers into believing they are totally inadequate to do research. As a consequence, many important problems in education have not really been solved; the experts distorted them to fit computerized models that esoteric approaches to research technology require.

CREDENTIALS AND JOB DESCRIPTIONS

Another product of the credentials myth is the organization of schools by job descriptions. Throughout the system, interminable discussions are carried on about the role of. . .—the role of the counselor, the role of the reading teacher, the role of the school nurse, the role of the assistant principal, etc., etc. When openings occur for new personnel, they are filled by first establishing job descriptions and then finding persons with credentials that fit those descriptions. Such an approach to staffing treats people and jobs as things, parts of a puzzle to be put together. Further, it assumes that persons and their credentials are synonymous.

People make an effective organization, not jobs. A good school or school system is one which has constructed its own peculiar gestalt so that all workers use themselves and their skills efficiently for the education of children. Workers' titles should be a totally irrelevant question. A glance around any system will quickly make it clear that jobs become what people make them. No matter what the job description, the person holding a position molds it to his or her own personality, skills, and beliefs. This is as it should be. Insistence upon job descriptions and the clear delineation of roles can seriously destroy morale and the effectiveness of the school system by encouraging internecine wars and continuous battles to establish and defend territorial rights.

SOME EFFECTS ON TEACHERS

The specialty-is-better syndrome has two other unhappy effects: (1) the denigration of the elementary teacher accompanied by the glorification of the subject matter specialist, and (2) the flight of the teacher from the classroom to specialist status.

The Teacher Put-down

Application of the credentials myth creates a hierarchy of value, prestige, and status. The college professor–research specialist is at the top of the heap followed by junior college and high school subject matter teachers with the elementary teacher at the very bottom. This hierarchy is also accompanied by a pecking order in which higher degrees of specialization may criticize or condemn with impunity those less specialized persons below. This puts the elementary teacher in the position of being "low man on the totem pole," criticized by everyone and generally regarded with disdain for dealing with "Mickey Mouse" matters. Such criticism is grossly unfair and destroys teacher morale. Elementary teachers cannot be specialists in subject matter; they have too many diverse responsibilities. Modern teacher-education programs for elementary teachers, for example, may require proficiency in reading, language arts, mathematics, science, social studies, music, art, children's literature, health, and physical education, to say nothing of psychology, curriculum, and social foundations. A good elementary teacher is required to know enough in each of these areas to start a child on the way up the educational ladder. To do the job well, the teacher must be an educational *generalist* on subject matter and a specialist in understanding children and how they learn.

The elementary teacher's skills may seem very simple to the outside observer, but so do the skills of any professional worker who knows his or her business and does it well. It is not at all uncommon to find elementary teachers who are doing a magnificent job putdown and scorned by specialists far less capable of handling their own professional responsibilities. Good elementary teachers deserve the highest respect and admiration, but the specialty myth too often relegates them to the cellar, rewards them with the lowest teacher salaries, and treats them as second-rate citizens.

Flight from the Classroom

A second effect the credentials myth has on teachers is the flight it produces from the classroom. The added prestige, status, and salary attached to specialist roles seduces hundreds of fine teachers from the classroom into jobs less necessary or less valuable for the primary purposes of education. They become victims of the "Peter Principle"—being promoted to their highest level of incompetence. As a consequence, a large number of first-rate teachers become second-rate administrators, and teachers who formerly encouraged and nurtured the growth of many become specialists confined to patch-up work for a few.

In government we've learned that military experts are not the best persons to handle international relations, nor are atomic physicists the right persons to decide on the uses of atomic power. In education, too, it is necessary to take a careful look at the experts. It's not necessarily true that industrialists, subject-matter specialists, researchers, administrators, or specialists of whatever variety are the best persons to make either the overall decisions, or the day to day ones, about curriculum and practice. I know elementary principals who say they would not have a guidance counselor in their school because a "guidance counselor is a specialist in human relations. When you have one around, teachers wash their hands of their problem children and pack them off to the experts." The position is extreme, to be sure; it also expresses a frustration that cannot be ignored.

Generally speaking, the greater the specialization, the narrower the perspective of the practitioner. What is required to adequately solve many human problems is not narrow specialization, but the broadest possible perspective from which to choose solutions. Unwarranted faith in credentials can result in abdication of responsibility by the very people who have the broader perspectives and are in the best positions to help. Of course, such passing of the buck and abandonment of responsibility can happen with any specialty—art, music, administration, supervision, special education, or counseling. Specialists are valuable and do have a place in education. School personnel need all the help they can get to aid the growth of children. The production of intelligent citizens requires intelligent, skillful, professional teachers. But myths that destroy teachers' faith in themselves, derogate human resources, or allocate decision making to the wrong persons, as does the credentials myth, are counter-productive.

Labels and credentials are no guarantee of performance. People's contributions to the process of schooling are dependent on who they are and what they can do with young people. The will and ability to help young people grow is too rare and too precious. An effective, efficient educational system must learn to make the fullest possible use of such talents no matter what they are called or where they are found.

SELECTED READINGS

Goodman, P. *Compulsory Mis-education.* New York: Horizon Press, 1964.

Illich, I. D. *Deschooling Society.* New York: Harper & Row, Publishers, 1971.

Postman, N., and Weingartner, C. *Teaching as a Subversive Activity.* New York: Delacorte Press, 1969.

Reimer, E. W. *School is Dead: Alternatives in Education.* Garden City, N.Y.: Doubleday & Company, Inc., 1971.

Silberman, C. *Crisis in the Classroom.* New York: Random House, Inc., 1970.

Waller, W. *The Sociology of Teaching.* New York: John Wiley & Sons, Inc., 1965.

The Myths of Objectivity and the Industrial Model

Several contemporary myths in our society have grown out of the industrial-scientific culture in which we live. Among these are the myths of objectivity and the myth of the industrial model. The first holds that all problems can be solved by logic and objectivity, the second that our experience applying those principles in industry will work everywhere else. We are currently trying to apply these myths to all aspects of education in the fond hope that they will make our schools more efficient. It is natural to expect the methods that have worked well in one place to do the same in others. If the new problems are truly like the old ones, this thinking may be accurate. If the new problems are fundamentally different, however, application of old techniques to new problems will not only fail to solve them, but it may create new ones. We are presently in that predicament as we try to apply the objective-industrial model to schools.

APPLYING THE OBJECTIVE–INDUSTRIAL MODEL TO EDUCATION

There is very good reason why our society admires objectivity so much. It has served us well in dealing with the world of "things" so important to our materialistic culture. Objectivity is in our blood. We carved our nation out of the wilderness, a problem in controlling things. We worship science as a sacred cow and, of course, the basic tenet of science is objectivity. The magnificent accomplishments of American industry, in supplying us with vast quantities of goods and services, were essentially achieved by objective approaches to production. Even our religions have taught us to regard ourselves as objects and have entreated us to make ourselves behave.

With such a background it is not surprising that when we are confronted with problems our first cry is likely to be, "Get the facts." When we have the facts, the belief goes, almost anything is possible by approaching the problem in a businesslike way. It is simply a matter of logic: one establishes objectives, analyzes the situation, creates a plan of action, puts it into operation, and measures the outcomes to determine whether it succeeded or not. This is the time-honored sequence by which breathtaking marvels of science and industry have been produced. It has served us well in controlling the world of things. It breaks down badly when applied to human beings.

People are not objects. They are thinking, feeling, perceiving, loving, hating, believing, striving, dynamic, *subjective* beings. They simply do not behave according to the facts as observed by outsiders. They behave according to their perceptions or beliefs, which may, or may not, correspond to the facts as others see them.

Our educational system is currently being subjected to the systematic application of objective-industrial model thinking in the hope of making schools more accountable. The goal of education must surely be "improved behavior" on the part of students. Logically, it would seem then, to improve education we need to determine the behaviors we wish to produce, activate the machinery to produce those behaviors, and then test the product to determine if, indeed, the goals were achieved. The reasonableness of this procedure seems unassailable. It is logical, straightforward, and objective. It is the technique we use for the solution of many of the problems we confront in our daily lives. As a consequence, objective techniques of management and control are being applied everywhere to educational problems.

Systems Approaches in Education

"Systems analysis," demands for behavioral objectives, PPBS programming, "perting," and computer controlled analyses of input and outcome are only a few of the techniques currently being applied to educational problems and practices. Even the language of industry is employed to describe educational processes. It is not uncommon to hear teaching described as "delivery systems," evaluation as "feedback" or "accounting," supervision as "monitoring," and classroom dynamics as questions of "input-output." We confidently expect that what has worked so well to improve industrial productivity will also improve education. The attempt is doomed to failure.

A system, it should be understood, is neither good nor bad in its own right. A systems approach is only a device to assure reaching stated objectives. If the objectives are good, a system will help achieve them. If the objectives are poor or inappropriate, a system will guarantee that errors will be colossal.

The goal of education is quite different from that of industry. For industry, the goal is production of a product. The worker is a cog in the process, the means by which the product is produced. For education, *the worker is the product*. The growth and welfare of the student is the goal. That is not an objective, but a deeply subjective problem. If industry were organized for the growth and welfare of its workers, rather than for the production of a product, it would surely be organized very differently.

People cannot be successfully dealt with in purely objective terms. Even in industry this fact is increasingly understood. For example, in the classic Hawthorne studies, investigators sought to find clues to improve productivity.[1] So, beginning from objective-logical premises, they systematically manipulated hours of work, illumination, rest periods, and many other conditions related to workers on the job. Each change in conditions, they found, produced an increase in productivity. The big surprise came when they decided to see what would happen if all these improvements were removed. Workers were returned to their original state and production went up still more! Apparently the workers' *feeling* that they were "special people" because they were involved in "an experiment" produced an increase in productivity no matter what was done to them.

It is fascinating (and dismaying) to note that even as education attempts to adopt the industrial model, many industries are having second thoughts about it. Some are experimenting with ways to modify time-honored assembly line concepts of production. Others are seeking ways to humanize working conditions, even to the point of including workers in decision making and management.[2]

Objective approaches to subjective problems can seriously interfere with, and even destroy, the possibilities for successfully dealing with many of our pressing human problems. But the myth of objectivity is very hard to combat. For a materialistic culture it has the illusion of being so logical, so straightforward, so businesslike, and so in line with all our past experiences that we come to believe it is universally applicable. We therefore continue to apply it everywhere, even to human problems for which it is not appropriate.

The blind adoption of techniques and practices that were successful in an institution with one set of goals to another institution with quite different goals can be highly destructive. Education is for the most part a subjective question, a *people* problem for which the myths of objectivity and the industrial model have only limited application. There are other more appropriate models for education derived from humanistic approaches to psychology and new understandings of the helping professions. Interested readers can find information about these developments in the works of such writers as Carl Rogers, Abraham Maslow, Earl Kelley, Arthur Combs, George Brown, James Bugental, and C. H. Patterson.[3] The humanistic approaches to psychology and education offered by such authorities provide new and exciting guidelines for educational practice. Many of the alternatives discussed in the remainder of this book are derived from their thinking.

NOTES

1. F. J. Roethlisberger and W. J. Dickson, *Management and the Worker* (Cambridge, Mass.: Harvard University Press, 1939).
2. A. J. Morrow, *Behind the Executive Mask* (New York: American Management Association, 1964); and A. J. Morrow, D. G. Bowers and S. E. Seashore, *Management by Participation* (New York: Harper & Row, Publishers, 1967).
3. *See* the Selected Readings directly following these Notes.

SELECTED READINGS

Association for Supervision and Curriculum Development. *To Nurture Humaneness: Commitment for the 70s* (1970 Yearbook). Washington, D.C.: Association for Supervision and Curriculum Development, 1970.

Bugental, J. F. T. *Challenges of Humanistic Psychology.* New York: McGraw-Hill, 1967.

Buhler, C., and Allen, M. *Introduction to Humanistic Psychology.* Belmont, Calif.: Wadsworth Publishing Co. Inc., 1972.

Combs, A. W., Richards, A. C., and Richards, F. *Perceptual Psychology: A Humanistic Approach to the Study of Persons.* New York: Harper & Row, Publishers, 1976.

Goble, F. G. *Third Force: The Psychology of Abraham Maslow.* New York: Grossman Publishers, 1970.

Laszlo, E. *The Systems View of the World.* New York: George Braziller, Inc., 1972.

Patterson, C. H. *Humanistic Education.* Englewood Cliffs, N.J.: Prentice-Hall, Inc., 1973.

Severin, F. T. *Humanistic Viewpoints in Psychology.* New York: McGraw-Hill, 1965.

Simpson, E. L. *Humanistic Education: An Interpretation.* Cambridge, Mass.: Ballinger Publishing Company, 1977.

Weinberg, Carl, ed. *Humanistic Foundations of Education.* Englewood Cliffs, N.J.: Prentice-Hall, Inc., 1972.

The Behavioral Objectives Myth

To make education more accountable, schools everywhere are going all out for behavioral objectives.[1] A behavioral objectives approach urges teachers to address their tasks in more businesslike ways through disciplined procedures for establishing objectives and assessing the outcomes of teaching. Teachers are required to clearly define their objectives in behavioral terms and establish performance criteria by which attainment can be judged.

The rationale behind this approach seems utterly sound. It is consistent with the scientific method we worship everywhere in our culture and with the hard-nosed assembly line procedures that have made our industries "models of production." This approach may be observed in managerial techniques like "systems analysis," "perting," "PPBS programming," "computer controlled production," and the like. The success of these schemes in increasing productivity in industry raises hope in the minds of many that they will have equally salutary effects on education.

LIMITATIONS OF BEHAVIORAL OBJECTIVES FOR EDUCATION

Unhappily, applying behavioral objectives to education proves deeply disappointing for several reasons:

1. Behavioral objectives concentrate on symptoms.
2. A behavioral objectives approach is a closed system approach to learning.
3. Preoccupation with behavioral objectives distorts the thrust of education.
4. Behavioral objectives are inadequate for humanistic goals.

Behavioral Objectives Concentrate on Symptoms

The behavior of an individual at any moment is not cause; it is result. Because people behave according to their perceptions of themselves and the world they are involved in, behavior at any instant is no more than a symptom of what is going on inside the individual—a result of some inner motivation. Basing educational planning on behavior is no more productive than only treating the symptoms of a disease while ignoring the causes behind them.

Failure to understand the symptomatic character of behavior has frustrated the efforts of educators to deal with learning problems for generations. If the teacher's attention is riveted on the child's behavior and the necessity to change it, instead of the reasons behind the behavior, techniques employed will almost certainly be manipulative attempts to control and direct the child's actions. These efforts may have to be repeated day after day after day if nothing has been done to deal with the basic causes of the behavior. Techniques of accountability that focus teacher attention upon the behavior of children may actually be directing teachers to look in the wrong place to effect important changes.

A Behavioral Objectives Approach Is a Closed System Approach to Learning

The behavioral objectives approach defines precise goals in advance and thereafter the task of the teacher is to manipulate events in such fashion as to bring students to those predetermined goals. This places a straightjacket on teachers and students alike and makes the learning situation essentially a search for "right" answers.[2] In its most extreme form teachers are required to set forth their objectives in exact behavioral terms, stating in advance the specific outcomes they expect. This approach is sometimes successful in the teaching of precisely defined skills such as arithmetic, reading, and writing, or in the production of uncomplicated behavior. But, as the student progresses, and the goals of teaching and learning become more complex and individual, the usefulness of behavioral objectives rapidly decreases.

Students taught in closed systems are very likely to feel trapped, caught in a mesh over which they have no control. Having no part in the determination of ends, they are not likely to feel a commitment to them. This leads, in turn, to the belief that schooling is irrelevant. Teachers may be regarded as "the enemy" and the school system as something to be sabotaged if possible.

A closed system of thinking also leads directly to a "great man" philosophy of education. Somebody must know where the people should go so others can arrange things to make sure they get there—a strange philosophy for schools in a democratic society. In a closed system, teachers must be all-knowing; there is no room to be wrong. They must be expert diagnosticians capable of dealing with thousands of contingencies. Such diagnosis is difficult enough for clinical psychologists who spend all their time at it; for most teachers it poses an impossible demand. Closed systems of thinking are all too likely to discourage innovation, stifle creativity, and make the classroom a dull, conforming place where people learn right answers to problems they don't have yet.

Preoccupation with Behavioral Objectives Distorts the Thrust of Education

While behavioral objectives are useful in the achievement of specific skills, they do not lend themselves effectively to more general objectives such as intelligent behavior, effective problem solving, creativity, responsibility, or good citizenship. To be used effectively, behavioral objectives must customarily be defined with great specificity. Teachers are exhorted to "be exact," "state your objectives precisely," "define what behavior you expect to produce." Such directives narrow the goals of teaching to ever smaller and smaller units that can be measured simply and so contribute further to the dehumanizing influence already rife in our educational system. By concentrating attention on specific, rather than general, goals of education, the major thrust of the entire system tends to be distorted as minor, rather than major, goals take precedence in the classroom.

This distortion is further compounded by the fact that behavioral objectives are likely to be determined by the nature of the measuring instruments available. Ideally, objectives should be established and methods of measurement then found or invented to test them. Too often the reverse is true. Objectives are formulated in terms of instruments readily at hand; matters for which there are no existing instruments are ignored. Overall goals of education become distorted so as to concentrate on producing behaviors we know how to measure. This tends to stifle innovation and divert attention from broader, holistic goals.

Behavioral Objectives Are Inadequate for Humanistic Goals

Learning basic skills is not the sole objective of education. People have always expected schools to contribute to the quality of human life. Throughout the history of education, every list of objectives established by professional educators, parents, or the general public has included such broad, humanistic goals as good citizenship, responsibility, worthy home membership, physical and mental health, concern for democratic values, creativity, and concern for other people. This is true right down to the last White House Conference on Education. Schools that do no more than teach people to read, write, and calculate will fail us all. Our society can get along much better with a bad reader or a bad mathematician than it can with an unintelligent citizen, or persons characterized by irresponsibility, dependence, hostility, or lack of concern for other people. Humanistic objectives are an absolute essential for the kind of society we live in.

By humanistic objectives modern educators mean:

1. **Holistic Objectives.** These are broad, general goals for human being and becoming. These goals include such characteristics as intelligent behavior, creativity, adaptability, responsibility, independence, autonomy, positive views of self, self-actualization, identification with others, and formulation of values and attitudes.

2. **Affective Objectives.** These have to do with aspects of learning involved in the student's discovery of personal meaning. (*See* the "Myth of the Affective Domain" on page 159.)

3. **Inner Life Objectives.** People are not mere cognitive machines. What makes us human are our feelings —the things we believe, hope, like, dislike, value, seek, and aspire to. An educational system that ignores these vital aspects of human experience has immensely narrowed its possibilities for significant impact. Worse still, because human feelings and values affect everything else that people learn, ignoring their effect on learning processes will decrease the school's success in dealing with cognitive matters. Students are human and that fact must be dealt with. No contemporary school can afford to overlook humanistic objectives. To do so is to deny the nature of the persons the system is designed to aid.

Humanistic objectives do not lend themselves readily to precise behavioral description. Intelligent behavior, for example, has to do with a person's ability to confront new problems and find effective, adequate solutions. If such solutions could be spelled out in advance, behavior would not be intelligent. Similarly, human feelings and the personal meaning of information do not lend themselves to measurement in behavioral terms. Preoccupation with behavioral objectives runs serious risk of distorting educational goals.

ACCOUNTABILITY

As our nation struggles to update its educational system, educators are being asked to stand accountable for the immense expenditures of human and financial resources for education. No one can really oppose the idea of accountability. Every institution must be held accountable and schools are no exception. It is possible, however, that the means we choose to achieve accountability may boomerang to destroy or impede the goals of education. Just as the production of a truly healthy person requires a balanced diet, the approaches we take to accountability must provide a balanced perspective for improving the health of education. Too much, even of a good thing, can destroy prime objectives. We cannot afford to let preoccupation with one or another system for achieving accountability destroy overall goals. Yet, that is precisely what is currently happening as we pour vast sums of money and the time and energies of thousands of persons into the behavioral objectives–performance criteria concept for achieving accountability.

Persons concerned with accountability must, themselves, be held accountable for the effects their current demands are having upon our educational system. Unthinking advocacy of behavioral objectives, no matter how well intended, is much too narrow a view of accountability. The behavioral objectives approach is not wrong. It would be easier to deal with if it were. The danger lies in that it is partly right. The behavioral objectives approach does, indeed, have limited value and often works quite effectively when applied to the acquisition of precisely defined skills. It, thus, has an important place in a system of accountability. Unfortunately, behavioral objectives also have such a logical, tangible quality that they are likely to create illusions of accuracy and efficiency far beyond the assistance they can actually deliver. As the sole or primary means for assessing educational outcomes, they leave very much to be desired. A proper approach to accountability must cover *all* objectives of education including humanistic ones. Anything less will leave us far short of our educational goals.

NOTES

1. Much of the material in this discussion is adapted from A. W. Combs, *Educational Accountability: Beyond Behavioral Objectives* (Washington, D.C.: Association for Supervision and Curriculum Development, 1972).
2. *See also:* the "Myth that Knowledge Is Stable" on page 77 and the "Fountainhead Myth" on page 185.

SELECTED READINGS

Bugental, J. F. T. *Challenges of Humanistic Psychology.* New York: McGraw-Hill, 1967.

Combs, A. W. "Can We Measure Good Teaching Objectively?" *NEA Journal* 53 (1964): 34–36.

Brown, G. J. *Human Teaching for Human Learning.* New York: The Viking Press, 1971.

Leonard, G. *Education and Ecstasy.* New York: Delacorte Press, 1968.

Orlich, D., and Ratcliff, J. "Coping with the Myth of Accountability." *Educational Leadership* 34 (1977): 246–52.

Wass, H. "Educational Accountability Here and Abroad." *Educational Leadership* (April 1972): 618–20.

The Law and Order Myth

We pride ourselves on being "a nation of laws, not men." When things go wrong we try to solve our problems by enacting new laws or redoubling efforts to enforce old ones. Sometimes this management philosophy works. More often, only the surface manifestations of problems are affected and our reliance on management procedures provides no more than the illusion that something is being done. Despite its frequent failures, the myth of law and order is offered again and again as an appropriate solution for the difficult problems faced not only in society, but in our schools as well. It finds expression in education as the myth of the value of punishment and the myth that there really is nothing a good flogging won't cure.

TWO APPROACHES TO BEHAVIOR

To deal with the law and order myth effectively, it is necessary to understand the two ways that are available to us for dealing with people. One way is to manage behavior. The other is to bring about change in the belief systems of persons.

The Management Approach

The management approach to behavior grows out of the psychological principle that people behave according to the

forces exerted upon them. This is readily observable by anyone looking around himself or herself. People pay their taxes
or else, buy advertised products, follow the boss's orders, and
generally react to pressures exerted upon them in innumerable
ways. It follows from such observations that the proper way
to solve human problems is to manipulate the stimuli or forces
acting on people. This principle naturally results in forms of
motivation that are dependent upon rewarding "right" behavior or punishing "wrong" behavior. It produces a kind of
fencing-in technique for controlling behavior like that used in
a stockyard to move cattle from one place to another. One
opens the gates where he or she wants the cattle to go and
closes those where he or she wants them kept out. Having
done this, moving cattle from one place to another is a simple
matter of exerting pressure from the rear to make them move
forward through the lane prepared. The method works fine for
cattle. It doesn't work well for people. People have an annoy-
ing habit of climbing over fences or discovering gates we for-
got to close.

There can be no doubt that the management philosophy
often works. There are times when all we want of people is
that they behave in some prescribed fashion. We want them
to stop for red lights and go for green ones, pay their bills,
leave other people's property alone, come to work on time,
send their children to school, or behave in a thousand other
precisely described ways. We don't really care what they feel
or think about the matter; what we want is proper behavior.
Unfortunately, management techniques work so well for such
problems, we assume they will work on anything. That's
where we get into trouble.

The Personal Approach

Behavior, as I have previously pointed out, is only a
symptom, the surface manifestation of what is going on inside
a person. The causes of behavior lie in people's beliefs, feel-

ings, understandings, hopes, values, and perceptions. These determine the things people do or do not do. Permanent behavior changes require alteration of these internal causative perceptions. Understanding the personal view of behavior provides an alternative way for dealing with human problems. It also suggests that when people change the way they see things, there may be no need to *control* behavior at all. For example, a small white child can be prevented from repeatedly hitting a black one by management techniques. The disruptive behavior in the classroom can be stopped by various forms of reward and punishment. But what happens outside the classroom, on the playground or in the neighborhood, is another matter. On the other hand, the obnoxious behavior of the white child may disappear entirely if some change is made in his perceptions. If he comes to see his black classmate as a person like himself, "a good kid to know and be friends with," control of the hitting behavior will no longer be necessary. It will disappear of itself.

The personal approach to human problems requires making some change in the belief system of the behaver. This is not easy for at least three reasons:

1. Since the causes of behavior lie within the person, they cannot be directly manipulated or changed. Outsiders can only influence, facilitate, or help changes to happen by the ways they themselves behave and the experiences they provide for the behaver.
2. Since the causes of behavior lie within the person, they are under his or her control. They cannot be changed without some sort of cooperation from the person whose behavior is to be changed.
3. Causes of behavior, like feelings, beliefs, understandings, attitudes, and values, do not change easily or quickly. The more important the perception in the value system of the behaver, the more difficult the process of change.

To produce a bountiful crop, a gardener plants the seed in the finest soil available, and then surrounds the growing plant with the very best possible conditions for growth. In the same way, the personal approach to learning provides the best possible environment for students to explore problems and discover solutions. It concentrates on processes of helping, facilitating, and assisting students rather than on direct control and management of specific behaviors. Using this less-contrived and less-managed approach does not mean that excellence in behavior is valued less. Quite the contrary. The personal approach is an alternate road to excellence more likely to achieve that goal in the long run.

SOME PROS AND CONS OF MANAGEMENT TECHNIQUES

Failure to understand the fundamental differences between the management and personal approaches to human behavior results in great frustration. Management techniques are only temporary. They keep breaking down and much energy has to be spent trying to repair or plug up one hole after another. This is a never ending process. Human ingenuity for finding loopholes is practically limitless. Despite hundreds of years devoted to designing escape-proof prisons, prisoners continue to find ways of getting out. We are surprised to discover that saturation bombing does not break the enemy's will, but strengthens their resistance. From kindergarten through graduate school, rules made to control behavior, no matter how cleverly designed, are no more than attractive challenges for students who quickly find ways of circumventing them.

Despite its inefficiency for the long haul, the management approach has many *seeming* advantages. Among these are:

1. It is direct. The target is clearly discernible as some specific behavior to be changed.

2. It is immediate. Results can be immediately observed and assessed.
3. Techniques can frequently be applied, with or without the recipient's consent.
4. It provides the user with a feeling of power and control. For many people these feelings afford such great personal satisfaction that they override all other considerations.

Despite these apparent advantages, the management approach provides only the illusion of effectiveness and efficiency. It seems simple, straightforward, and businesslike, and for many it is the only approach they know or understand. The personal approach, while it is more difficult, is often more effective. It takes more time and understanding. It calls for techniques of helping, facilitating, aiding, teaching, and encouraging. For many problems in education, it is the better approach.

THE NEED FOR PERSONAL
APPROACHES IN EDUCATION

Management approaches are sometimes necessary in classrooms just as they are in society at large. The objectives of education, however, run far beyond the immediate behavior of students. Schools must be concerned with long-term outcomes: permanent changes in student beliefs, attitudes, feelings, values, and understandings; intelligent behavior; creativity; responsibility; and autonomy of action. Management approaches, however valuable for accomplishing short-term goals, are inadequate for efficiently achieving many long-term goals. Teachers and administrators must know and understand *both* the management and personal approaches to helping students grow. Different problems require different tools. Teachers restricted to a single approach are at a great disadvantage.

The point of view we adopt when we confront a problem

inevitably determines what we do to solve it. The management approach and the personal approach have quite different built-in consequences. For example, the teacher looking at a child's misbehavior from a management point of view thinks, "That behavior must stop." The teacher's actions thereafter are directed toward marshalling the forces necessary to stop the objectionable behavior, usually some form of reward or punishment. Looking at the same disruptive behavior from a personal approach, the teacher may conclude, "That child feels people don't like him very well." Such a perception of the situation calls for an entirely different constellation of strategies; helping a child feel better about himself or herself is very different from controlling and directing that child's behavior.

Good teachers, of course, utilize *both* approaches; they utilize management techniques for immediate problems and personal methods for long-term ones. Poor teachers are often restricted to one approach or the other, never getting beyond the immediate problems of maintaining law and order or being so concerned with the human touch that immediate problems get out of hand.

SOME EFFECTS OF
PREOCCUPATION WITH
LAW AND ORDER

Every aspect of a school and its operations are affected by the orientation of its administrators and teachers to the management approach or the personal approach. Schools totally committed to the myth of law and order may be so successful at producing student conformity that they frustrate long-term objectives such as intelligent behavior, responsibility, and creativity. Predicating action on the myth of law and order alone also affects student and teacher morale, communication, human interrelationships, working conditions, and community-school cooperation and support. More important than school operation is how the management approach affects what students learn about themselves, their relations with other people, and desirable ways of behaving in the larger society. Students learn these things, not from what they are told, but from the examples they are set. Constant exposure to management techniques yields a lopsided view of how to behave as a citizen, how to solve social problems, and how to judge the behavior of others.

Truly adequate education must equip youth with the widest possible understandings and skills for problem solving. To do this, educators must understand and use *both* management and personal approaches to problem solving. Schools cannot afford a preoccupation with the myth of law and order. They must also apply personal, humanistic approaches to understanding and teaching young people.

SELECTED READINGS

Amos, W. E., and Orem, R. C. *Managing Student Behavior.* St. Louis: Green Publishing Co., 1967.

Combs, A. W. "Two Views of Motivation." *Handbook of Research on Motivation.* By J. F. Frymeir. Columbus, Ohio: Ohio State University Press, 1971.

Hitt, W. D. "Two Models of Man." *American Psychologist* 24 (1969): 651–58.

Marrow, A. J. *Behind the Executive Mask.* New York: American Management Association, 1964.

Plank, E. L. "Violations of Children's Rights in the Classroom." *Childhood Education* 52 (1975): 73–75.

Rogers, C. *Freedom to Learn.* Columbus, Ohio: Charles E. Merrill Publishing Co., 1969.

Rogers, C. R., and Skinner, B. F. "Some Issues Concerning the Control of Human Behavior." *Science* 24 (1956): 1057–1066.

Skinner, B. F. *Beyond Freedom and Dignity.* New York: Bantam Books, Inc., 1972.

The Attack–Appease Myth

Public reaction to confrontation is usually to reduce alternatives for solution to a dichotomy—attack or appease. According to this thinking, difficult social problems can be dealt with either by forcing our will upon others or by giving in to what others demand. These are the options suggested for such confrontations as riots, college student sit-ins, civil rights marches, draft evasions, Indian claims to valuable land, or conservationists blocking the bulldozers at a new dam site. Such precarious thinking is even applied to international problems where stakes can escalate to ultimate choices between war or capitulation. A concept so prevalent in larger society cannot help but carry over to its institutions. The attack–appease myth inevitably finds expression in schools. It shows itself everywhere, in relations between teachers and students and between administrators and teachers, in contract negotiations, in public relations, and in interscholastic sports, to name a few.

If it is true, as many would have us believe, that we have only two choices, attack or appease, then we are in a fearsome dilemma. If we appease, we not only lose the issue at stake, but we lose our own dignity and integrity as well. On the other hand, if we attack, we are put in the morally indefensible position of being the bully or despot, a position repugnant to essentially peace loving people. Either way we lose. This is the unsavory choice we are offered for dealing with problems both in and out of school. What's more, there are many who would tell us there is no alternative.

AN ALTERNATE CHOICE

Is there an alternative to appeasement or attack? I believe there is and feel we need to be clearly and sharply aware of it, lest we become the unwitting victims of our own misconceptions. This alternative is an approach that social scientists have discovered to be basic to good human relationships everywhere. It is not so much an alternative to attack or appeasement as it is an approach on a different axis altogether. It says in effect: "I am a person of dignity and integrity. I stand four square in the security of my fundamental beliefs. I have no need to attack you nor will I permit you to attack me. I do not fear you and I will not give you cause to fear me." This is a position that is neither attack nor appeasement. It is not concerned with winning or losing. It is focused, instead, on the maintenance of human integrity and the preservation of freedom for people to grow and develop. Appeasement destroys the dignity of the appeaser. Attack violates the integrity of others. This alternative position maintains the dignity and integrity of individuals without violating their own rights or those of others. It is a position of strength and security that stands *for* something as well as against something.

This position is by no means new. It is the method of Schweitzer, and Ghandi, and, to a lesser degree, of all of us in our better moments. We all know people who behave this way. Now and then we collectively rise to our full stature and behave this way as a nation.

Strangely enough, in spite of its age-old character, this method of dealing with people is an approach without a name. This is a great tragedy, because we cannot deal effectively with matters that do not have clear terms by which we can refer to them. Attack and appease are unequivocal and easily understood. As a result they come easily and quickly to mind when we are confronted with a problem. We need an equally sharp and distinctive term for the kind of relationship described here. Perhaps we shall find one in time. For the sake of this book, let's call it *the humane approach*.

Modern psychology has found the humane approach to be characteristic of well-adjusted people. Studies of self-actualized personalities show they have strong feelings of dignity and integrity.[1] They respect themselves and have high degrees of respect for other persons. Conversely, a major characteristic of poorly adjusted people is a lack of respect for self, and an inability to accept one's self as is. Effective, well-adjusted personalities are people with well-conceived convictions and beliefs. Because they have such convictions, they are far less threatened by other people and have much less need to attack. They are much more willing to see things clearly and unambiguously as they are and to admit what is so without fear, anger, or the necessity for self-delusion. They accept themselves as people of dignity and integrity and they treat others as people of dignity and integrity too.

THE EFFECTS OF THREAT
ON BEHAVIOR

Threat stands in the way of the humane approach. When people feel threatened, they are less able to handle problems effectively. Experiencing threat results in defense of self and produces tunnel vision.

Threat Forces Defense of Self

When they feel threatened, people are forced to defend themselves. In a confrontation, this usually takes the form of threatening one's opponent. As a consequence, a vicious circle of threat and counterthreat may become established. The longer such conflict goes on, the faster and more intensively the spiral of threat and counterthreat rises. If not resolved, it can break out in violence and the complete breakdown of communication.

Threat Produces Tunnel Vision

Psychologists have found that when people feel threatened, their perceptions become narrowed to the threatening object. This is an effect familiar to all of us. We remember, for example, the automobile accident in which the only thing we could see was "that big truck coming at me." An example in education is the child in school who is worried about what is happening to his mother and is therefore unable to concentrate on anything else.

Threat and its effects, the necessity for self-defense and the narrowing of perceptions, make conflict difficult to resolve once it is well under way. They can have disastrous consequences for any school situation.

THE HUMANE APPROACH
IN EDUCATION

An unchecked spiral of threat and counterthreat between teachers and students can only end in the reduction of one of the combatants to impotence, a position in which one or the other is no longer threatening. The alternative, taking the humane approach, is to behave in ways that reduce the feelings of threat in ourselves and in our opponents. To achieve such strength requires a clear and consistent set of beliefs about one's self, one's purposes, and the nature of other people. Such personal frames of reference are shown in research to be characteristic of highly effective teachers.[2] They are acquired through continuous processes of examining and reexamining fundamental beliefs, making them ever clearer, more accurate, precise, and consistent. Firm beliefs and convictions are the best guarantees of consistent behavior toward other people. Personal convictions and beliefs also eliminate tunnel vision. Teachers will not be easily panicked by outside pressures; instead, they will be far more likely to understand and communicate with others. This, in turn, will cause others to trust them more because their behavior is stable and predictable.

The humane approach in education is a position of strength. It arises from a sincere belief in self and in the dignity and integrity of human beings—beliefs our democratic way of life is based on. The humane position is realistic and practical. It is a means by which we can resist aggression without becoming aggressors. We can grant others their rights and privileges without running the risk of appeasement. It is a position in which principles come first and expediency second.

The humane approach in education is a position worth holding. Like everything worth having, however, it can only be achieved at a price. It may sometimes require living with unsolved problems. Immediate solutions to human problems are not always possible to find. Sometimes it is necessary to live with unhappy and distressing situations while working out more adequate solutions. But attack and appeasement have price tags too. Because they are expedients, they are often quicker. In the long run they are also far more expensive in time, money, and the sacrifice of human dignity and integrity, a price education can hardly afford.

NOTES

1. *See,* for example, A. H. Maslow, *Motivation and Personality* (New York: Harper & Row, Publishers, 1970); and A. W. Combs, ed., *Perceiving, Behaving, Becoming,* 1962 Yearbook (Washington, D.C.: Association for Supervision and Curriculum Development, 1962).

2. *See* the following research:
   Robert G. Brown, "A Study of the Perceptual Organization of Elementary and Secondary Outstanding Young Educators"

(unpublished doctoral dissertation, University of Florida, 1970);

Chunghoon Choy, "The Relationship of College Teacher Effectiveness to Conceptual Systems Orientation and Perceptual Orientation" (unpublished doctoral dissertation, University of Northern Colorado, 1969);

A. W. Combs, *Florida Studies in the Helping Professions,* Social Science Monograph No. 37 (Gainesville, Fl.: University of Florida Press, 1969);

Charles Van Loan Dedrick, "The Relationship Between Perceptual Characteristics and Effective Teaching at the Junior College Level" (unpublished doctoral dissertation, University of Florida, 1972);

Donald A. Dellow, "A Study of the Perceptual Organization of Teachers and Conditions of Empathy, Congruence, and Positive Regard" (unpublished doctoral dissertation, University of Florida, 1971);

Eunice J. Doyle, "The Relationship Between College Teacher Effectiveness and Inferred Characteristics of the Adequate Personality" (unpublished doctoral dissertation, University of Northern Colorado, 1969);

Gerald Douglas Jennings, "The Relationship Between Perceptual Characteristics and Effective Advising of University Housing Para-Professional Residence Assistants" (unpublished doctoral dissertation, University of Florida, 1973);

B. Koffman, "A Comparison of the Perceptual Organizations of Outstanding and Randomly Selected Teachers in 'Open' and 'Traditional' Classrooms" (unpublished doctoral dissertation, University of Massachusetts, 1975);

Robert E. Morgenstern, "The Relationship Between Two Modes of Interpersonal Conditions and College Teacher Effectiveness" (unpublished doctoral dissertation, University of Northern Colorado, 1969);

Anne O'Roark, "A Comparison of Perceptual Characteristics of Elected Legislators and Public School Counselors Identified as Most and Least Effective" (unpublished doctoral dissertation, University of Florida, 1975);

Lois P. Picht, "Self-Concept in Relation to Effectiveness in Student Teaching" (unpublished doctoral dissertation, University of Northern Colorado, 1969);

Richard Usher and John Hanke, "Third Force in Psychology and College Teacher Effectiveness Research at the University of Northern Colorado," *Colorado Journal of Educational Research* 10 (Winter 1971): p. 2;

Herman G. Vonk, "The Relationship of Teacher Effectiveness to Perception of Self and Teaching Purposes" (unpublished doctoral dissertation, University of Florida, 1970).

SELECTED READINGS

Buber, M. *I and Thou.* New York: Charles Scribner's Sons, 1970.

Deutsch, M. *The Resolution of Conflict: Constructive and Destructive Processes.* New Haven, Conn.: Yale University Press, 1973.

Maslow, A. H. *Toward a Psychology of Being.* New York: Van Nostrand, 1962.

Renshon, S. A. *Psychological Needs and Political Behavior.* New York: The Free Press, 1974.

Roethlisberger, F. J. "Barriers to Communication Between Men." *The Use and Misuse of Language.* By S. I. Hayakawa. Greenwich, Conn.: Fawcett, 1962.

The Myths that If It's Hard, It's Good for You and Kids Won't Learn Unless You Make 'Em

IF IT'S HARD, IT'S GOOD
FOR YOU

It is not surprising that a nation which carved itself out of the wilderness should staunchly believe in the value of hard work and the nobility of struggle. It was the road to success for our early settlers. Couple that with a real sense of admiration most of us have for the courage demonstrated by persons suffering from handicaps and it is an easy jump to the belief that suffering necessarily results in refinement of character. The idea, if it's hard it must be good for you, is a myth, but one supported even by the stamp of religious authority. It was a basic concept of the austere church doctrines held by many of our early settlers. Its application in our public schools has caused incredible damage to millions of young people. It has been used to justify the most dismal curricula, boring instruction, and barbarous practices of discipline and control.

Struggle, in itself, has no value whatsoever. While it's true that some people have learned and grown as a consequence of struggle, millions more have been handicapped or ruined by confrontation with problems that proved too much for them. Difficulty, in its own right, is neither good nor bad. It is how the person dealing with the difficulty interprets the experience that makes it beneficial or detrimental.

A simple look around us at our culture should make it abundantly clear how false the idea of the value of struggle actually is. If it were true that struggle against insuperable odds was the high road to nobility, then surely our poor, deprived, and rejected citizens would be the very bulwark of our nation instead of the problem they often are. Occasionally, some stalwart individual arises out of the morass of deprivation to achieve despite his or her background. This provides new support for the myth that if it's hard it's good for you, but it is an exception. For the vast majority of our deprived citizens, the problems they confront are overwhelming, so much so that the result is often expressed in the apathy of despair or the violence of revolt.

Challenge and Threat

Psychologists make an important distinction between challenge and threat in human perception. Challenge is a positive experience. Its effects are highly motivating and its outcomes are likely to be rewarding and productive of maximum growth. Threat, on the other hand, is a negative experience producing the narrowness of tunnel vision and the immobility of self-defense. (*See* the "Attack–Appease Myth" on page 63.) Both these outcomes of threat are directly contrary to the goals of education. Education must broaden perspective, not narrow it, and must encourage change, not generate defense of the status quo.

People feel challenged when they are confronted with problems that interest them and that they believe they have a reasonable chance of handling successfully. People feel threatened when they are confronted with tasks that seem to them to be beyond their capacities. Whether a person is challenged or threatened is not a matter of how an outsider perceives the situation, but how the person involved perceives it. Similarly, whether a student is being threatened or challenged at any moment is not a question of how the teacher sees it, but how the student sees it. To accomplish its goals, education must find ways of challenging students without threatening them.

Problem Solving Leads to Growth

People grow by solving problems, not problems that are too much for them, but problems they perceive to be within their abilities to solve. Under those conditions, tasks may not be regarded as hard at all. Quite the contrary; they may be seen as fun—challenging, exciting, soul satisfying steps to personal fulfillment. Research on supremely healthy, self-actualizing persons finds them possessed of deep feelings of personal security achieved as a consequence of essentially successful experience.

The lesson from this for schools is not that tasks should be hard, but that tasks must be relevant. Problems must fit the peculiar needs and capabilities of individual students. This principle is called *pacing*, adjusting the level of tasks to the readiness of the learner. When the adjustment is done well, no one complains about tasks being too hard. Students are too busy doing what seems relevant and meaningful to raise the question even when they are involved with tasks that appear very difficult to an outside observer.

KIDS WON'T LEARN UNLESS YOU MAKE 'EM

A corollary to the if-it's-hard-it's-good-for-you myth is the myth that kids won't learn unless you make 'em. As usual, this myth contains a germ of truth. Children won't readily learn what they think is irrelevant or without personal meaning. But then, neither will anyone else. We all resist what we think has no value. On the other hand, we will work very hard, without coercion of any sort, to achieve a goal that seems personally worthwhile.

The myth that kids won't learn unless you make 'em probably came about as a consequence of attempts to force an irrelevant curriculum on students. Seeing no meaning in what they were asked to learn, students were not motivated to learn; they were turned off by the tasks they were asked to perform. From their point of view, it took a lot of effort to make themselves work under such conditions. Small wonder they claimed it was "too hard." Teachers, on the other hand, confronted with unwilling learners, found it necessary to increase the pressures to *make* the students learn. So the behaviors of students and teachers, acting and reacting to each other, created a disastrous circle confirming the myth that learning is hard for the students and the myth that kids won't learn unless you make 'em for the teachers.

When students feel challenged, even the most difficult tasks (seen from an outsider's point of view) may be tackled with gusto. As anyone who has ever watched a child learning to roller skate can attest, even physical pain can be cheerfully taken in stride if the goals to be reached are seen as desirable and enhancing. We need only examine our own experiences to find numerous instances refuting the concept that learning must be forced if it is to occur at all. For most of us, once we are out of school, the extensive learning achieved during the rest of our lives rarely, if ever, occurs as a result of force and coercion.

Whatever their origins, the myths that if it's hard it's good for you and kids won't learn unless you make 'em are serious handicaps to effective educational practice. Actions based on such false perceptions are self-fulfilling. Belief that learning must be hard and that students must be forced to learn can only result in creating conditions that turn students off. Innovations based on such self-destructive assumptions are ineffective. To achieve the educational changes we need, innovations must be based upon the clearest, most accurate conceptions about learners and the learning process possible in our times. Kids will learn difficult things without the use of coercion if what must be learned is (1) relevant to the present needs of the student, (2) paced to current status and capacity, and (3) interesting and rewarding to the learner. Educational practice based upon these basic principles will be far more likely to achieve results over the long haul.

SELECTED READINGS

Brown, G. I. *Human Teaching for Human Learning.* New York: The Viking Press, 1971.

Combs, A. W. *Perceiving, Behaving, Becoming* (1962 Yearbook). Washington, D.C.: Association for Supervision and Curriculum Development, 1962.

Hamilton, N. K., and Saylor, J. G. *Humanizing the Secondary School.* Washington, D.C.: Association for Supervision and Curriculum Development, 1969.

Holt, J. C. *Freedom and Beyond.* New York: E. P. Dutton & Co., Inc., 1972.

LaBenne, W. D., and Greene, B. I. *Educational Implications of Self-concept Theory.* Pacific Palisades, Calif.: Goodyear Publishing Co., Inc., 1969.

Manning, D. *Toward a Humanistic Curriculum.* New York: Harper & Row, Publishers, 1971.

Milgram, S. *Obedience to Authority.* New York: Harper & Row, Publishers, 1974.

Neill, A. S. *Summerhill.* New York: Hart Publishing Co., Inc., 1960.

The Myth that Knowledge Is Stable

Most people conceive of knowledge as being what human beings have learned through the course of history—that body of information, understanding, and experience accumulated by a particular culture. Knowledge is also regarded as highly stable stuff that may be increased over the years by additions of new experience but does not change much.

The belief that knowledge is stable is a myth, but it has resulted in the establishment of schools to "transmit the accumulated culture" and "to prepare students to assume their roles as responsible citizens." Such schools are chained to the past and prepare young people for a world that does not exist even in the present, and certainly not in the future. Once, schools could be designed on the assumption of a stable body of knowledge and so achieve a modicum of success in preparing youth for the world they would live in. But those days are gone forever. Two things are happening in the world we live in that guarantee we can never again base our thinking on the concept of a stable society or the certainty of a body of knowledge. These are: (1) the information explosion, and (2) the ever accelerating pace of change.

THE INFORMATION EXPLOSION

In today's world, an enormous amount of knowledge is available to us. In his book, *The Dynamics of Change*, Don Fabun tells us:

> We are told 25 percent of all the people who ever lived are alive today; that 90 percent of all the scientists that ever lived are living now; the amount of technical information available doubles every ten years; throughout the world, about 100,000 journals are published in more than 60 languages, and the number doubles every 15 years. We are told these things but we do not always act as if we believe them. [1]

The explosion of information, alone, makes it absolutely certain that our schools will never again be able to devise a curriculum required of everyone. The available knowledge from which we would have to choose a common curriculum is so great, any sample we settled on could not hope to prepare students for effective living in our modern complex society. The world has become so extraordinarily complex and needs so many different kinds of people to run it, the hope of providing a common curriculum even minimally appropriate for all has disappeared forever.

THE RAPIDITY OF CHANGE

The body of knowledge available to us is not simply expanding, it is also changing so rapidly that what is "so" today may be "not so" tomorrow. We need but review our own life spans to discover how rapidly things have changed even in that short period. The pace of change is incredibly fast and becoming much faster all the time.

It's clear that an educational system preoccupied with the past and preparing youth for a stable society in the future must surely fail its responsibilities. As Alvin Toffler points out: "All education springs from some image of the future. If the image of the future held by society is grossly inaccurate, its educational system will betray its youth." [2] Since we cannot know the requirements of the society of tomorrow, the age-old assumptions upon which we have built our educational system are no longer adequate. New goals are called for.

NEW GOALS FOR EDUCATION

Intelligent Behavior

The society of the future must be created "on the spot" by the citizens living in those times. The educational system required to prepare youth for such responsibilities will need to be very different from that we have known. Its objectives must shift from emphases upon subject matter, techniques, and answers to emphasis upon the production of *adaptable, problem-solving persons* who are capable of highly intelligent behavior. This change in goals will not be easy; institutions are notoriously intransigent to change and traditions have built-in inertia. Nevertheless, the demand for change is inexorable. If we cannot clearly define the future, our only alternative is to prepare young people as best we can to deal with any problem they may find when they get there.

"The ultimate purpose of futurism in education," says Alvin Toffler, "is not to create elegantly complex, well-ordered, accurate images of the future, but to help learners cope with real-life crises, opportunities, and perils. It is to strengthen the individual's practical ability to anticipate and adapt to change, whether through invention, informed acquiescence, or through intelligent resistance." [3] Schools emphasizing adaptable, intelligent behavior require person-centered curricula designed to help students behave in ever more intelligent ways. Such a goal would have been considered impossible when intelligence was regarded as a static hereditary quality not open to change. We now know better. Modern psychology tells us that intelligence can be created and supplies us with a list of factors through which that goal can be achieved. (*See* the "Myth of Fixed Intelligence" on page 105.) People can be helped to behave more intelligently both now and in the future by increasing the richness, extent, and availability of their experience. This can be done in the present even if we cannot foresee the peculiar problems to which that intelligence will be applied in the future.

Problem Solving

To meet the challenge of the unknown future, our educational system must concentrate on the improvement of problem-solving skills. To do this will require perceiving subject matter, not as an end in itself, but as the means through which problem solving skills can be learned. Such a view will require considerable expansion of the narrow curricula currently conceived to be the legitimate subject matter of schools. If problem solving is the primary goal, then *any* subject can provide an effective vehicle for learning and the criterion for selection will be in very large part whatever turns students on. The interest and commitment of students will become more important than the topics confronted.

A Continuously Changing Self

Human beings must change to live effectively in a world of rapid change. To prepare for that world, students need to grow up learning to cope with and adapt to change. Static, unchanging persons wedded to outmoded beliefs and concepts are a drag upon society at best. A population resistant to change can even be dangerous for a society facing new problems, techniques, or conceptions of human need. Such failures of society to adapt are the stuff from which wars and revolutions are manufactured. To be prepared for the world they must enter, students must learn how to change themselves, how to adapt to changing conditions, and how to maintain open-mindedness, toleration of ambiguity, and resistance to narrow or dichotomous concepts of what is right and proper. In the world of tomorrow, a bigot may be far more dangerous than a bad reader.

A curriculum designed to help young people change must concentrate on the student and what is happening to him or her. For generations, the major task of schools has been to help students confront "the accumulated culture." The school of the future must shift its attention to what is happening within the student himself or herself. Growing up must be understood as a continuous process of self-exploration and discovery. Responsibility, self-direction, autonomy, participation in decision-making, and planning must be an integral part of everyday experience. The student's awareness of what is happening within himself or herself must be emphasized more than the study of what has happened in the past or is happening now. Schools have a lot to learn about how to deal with such objectives. A major housecleaning is called for and the time is long overdue.

The Exploration of Values

In a world of rapidly changing facts and conditions, adequate decisions cannot be made in purely empirical terms. Action must be based on values and purposes that govern the choices people make from the kaleidoscope of changes occurring about them. Individual decisions about what is really important must provide the basis for discrimination. If human beings are to avoid being drowned or controlled by the onrush of change, they will need usable guidelines for reading the price tags attached to alternatives, for determining optimal directions, and for selecting effective means of achieving ends. This calls for clear and consistent value systems. They can be achieved through personal exploration and as a consequence of continuous personal confrontation, experimentation, and choice.

Value objectives, like worthy home-membership, belief in democratic values, and concern for other people, have always been general objectives of American education. They have also been generally ignored by the traditional preoccupation with subject matter and skills. The idea that our public schools should be concerned with students' values is still anathema to many people who regard such objectives as unwarranted meddling in the responsibilities of home and church or dangerous digressions from the proper task of schools to teach facts and skills. Much of this opposition stems from talk of "teaching values" which seems to imply indoctrination of students with some ready-made concept or dogma and so smacks of brainwashing or sinister subversion of youth. Most Americans have been opposed to such shenanigans at least as far back as the Declaration of Independence.

It is not a proper task of schools to "teach values" in the sense of inculcating someone's conception of the right ones. However, a school that does not aid its young people in the exploration of values has grossly failed its responsibilities. And, in fact, nothing can be taught without the involvement of values. (*See* the "Myth of the Affective Domain" on page 159.) The very choice of subject, textbook, lesson plan, or teaching practice is a valuing process and students go right on thinking and feeling and behaving with respect to their own values no matter what. Values and their consideration is a part of every classroom, whether teachers and public like it or not, because learning itself is a valuing process.

In a world of accelerating change, human values must provide directions for human decisions. If schools are to meet the challenge of preparing youth to live in that world, the exploration of values must become a major educational objective. We cannot afford the luxury of arguing about whether values are appropriate matters for educational concern. The accelerating pace of change has reduced that argument to absurdity. Education for the future will deal with values or miserably fail its students. The question we face is not "should we?" but "how?"

NOTES

1. Kaiser Aluminum & Chemical Corporation, "Dynamics of Change," © 1967. First appeared in *Kaiser News*, 1966. Included in Don Fabun, *The Dynamics of Change* (Englewood Cliffs, N.J.: Prentice-Hall, Inc., 1967), pp. 4–5.
2. Alvin Toffler, ed., *Learning for Tomorrow: The Role of the Future in Education* (New York: Random House, Inc., 1974), p. 3.
3. Ibid.

SELECTED READINGS

Chase, S. *The Most Probable World.* New York: Harper & Row, Publishers, 1968.

Green, T., ed. *Educational Planning in Perspective.* Schenectady, N.Y.: IPC Science and Technology Press, 1971.

Sarason, S. B. *The Culture of the School and the Problem of Change.* Boston: Allyn and Bacon, Inc., 1971.

Toffler, A. *Future Shock.* New York: Random House, Inc., 1970.

Toffler, A., ed. *Learning for Tomorrow: The Role of the Future in Education.* New York: Vintage Books, 1974.

Worth Commission on Educational Planning. *A Future of Choices: A Choice of Futures.* Edmonton, Canada: Hurtig, 1972.

PART II

MYTHS ABOUT THE NATURE OF PERSONS

Education is a people business charged with the responsibility of contributing to the growth and development of young people into effective, responsible citizens. Its goals and practices must, therefore, be based on the very best possible conceptions about what people are like and how they grow. If these basic conceptions are accurate, possibilities are open for education to make steady progress toward its goals. If they are false or inaccurate, the educational system is practically certain to fail. The beliefs educators hold about persons and their behavior are crucial. Education must rely heavily on the social sciences of psychology, sociology, and anthropology to provide clear understandings of the nature of persons and how they grow and develop.

Many conceptions about the nature of persons and their behavior go far back in human history. They came into being as a consequence of people's observations of what went on around them. When such ideas were accurate, they led to progress; when they were false, they often resulted in tragedy. Examples were the concept that mental illness was the result of being possessed by the devil and the belief that "ours is the one, true faith."

Some ancient myths about the nature of persons have been dispelled by new understandings modern science has provided. Some, however, are still alive, well, and operating all around us. Still others, believe it or not, have been created by the sciences themselves or by the interpretations people have made about scientific theory. Whatever their origins, false beliefs about people have inevitable effects on education. People trying to improve educational goals and practices need to be keenly aware of contemporary myths, lest those myths bind and frustrate well-intentioned efforts.

This part is designed to explore a number of myths about the nature of persons and their behavior toward one another. In Part III we will examine more closely a number of myths specific to modern educational structures.

The Myth that the Human Organism Can't Be Trusted

As people observed each other's behavior down through the ages, it was clear that sometimes people behaved well and sometimes people behaved badly. It was a natural jump, therefore, to assume that man is good and evil by nature. Some religious groups even went much farther to claim that people were originally conceived in sin and so must spend the rest of their lives learning to be good. Some philosophers, on the other hand, like Thoreau, regarded the organism as basically good, only becoming evil as a consequence of forces exerted on it by the world it lived in. Out of such observations and philosophies came the belief that the human organism is a kind of battleground where continuous warfare between good and bad impulses is waged. Even in modern times this belief has been given further credence; Freud and his followers, for example, pictured man as fundamentally motivated by the dark and mysterious id that was only kept in check by the forces of the super ego.

The myth that the human organism can't be trusted views human beings as bundles of sinful impulses ready to surge into action unless carefully held in check by some inner or outer forces. This belief is widely held in our society and has inevitable expression in our public schools. All kinds of coercion are justified by this myth. Freedom is restricted for fear students will get out of control. Rules, regulations, and authoritarian practices are freely employed because "all hell will break loose if you don't." Most people just don't believe that the human organism is trustworthy or dependable, so every effort is expended to surround it with controls designed to prevent it from sliding back into its fundamental bestial quality. As a result, the accepted mode of dealing with youth is to fence them in—decide what they should do, set up the machinery to assure they will do it, and then check on them again and again to make certain they did it. Such ways of dealing with youth seem eminently reasonable, approached from the myth of the untrustworthy organism. In reality, they are fallacious, inhibitive, and even destructive to human growth and development.

THE HUMANISTIC VIEW
OF PERSONAL MOTIVE

Modern humanistic psychology takes a quite different view of the nature of human beings. It does not see people as either good or bad. They just are. The basic impulse of all living things, humanists tell us, is to live as effectively as possible, to move toward fulfillment or health if the way is open to do so. This striving toward self-actualization is by no means haphazard and is characteristic of every form of life from the simplest cell to the most complex plant or animal. The single-celled amoeba flowing about in a drop of water moves *toward* food and *away* from danger if it can. The protoplasm of which it is composed has direction and that direction is toward fulfillment and health. Flowers bent by the rain and the wind stand up again if they can. In time, tree bark grows over the damage done by lightning. Dogs injured in one leg learn to run on three. People, too, have incredible powers of recovery from even the most serious injuries. Wherever we look, the prime impulse of life at every level seems singlemindedly intent on fulfillment and health.

The practice of medicine is based on the need of the organism to move toward health. No doctor ever cured a patient of anything. Doctors minister to the body, helping to create the conditions that will set its innate drive free to move toward health again. They may do this by eliminating the microorganisms causing a disease, by removing diseased or damaged tissues, or by building up the organism's resistance through diet or rest. In the final analysis, however, the body gets well of itself. Counselors, psychiatrists, psychologists, and social workers also depend on this drive to provide the motive for their clients and patients to move toward health and fulfillment. Good teachers do, too.

Barriers to Fulfillment

Modern humanistic thinking tells us that the human organism is completely trustworthy. It can, it will, it *must* move toward health and fulfillment if the way is open to do so. The *if* is the hooker. *If* the way is open, the organism can be depended upon to move. Unfortunately, many barriers can obstruct such movement. The following are among the factors that may prevent operation of a person's innate drive toward self-actualization:

1. **Lack of Necessary Knowledge About What Possibilities Exist.** Learning expands one's areas of maneuver. Stupidity and ignorance narrow and restrict one's choices.

2. **Lack of Awareness of, or Resistance to, Experience.** These may impede an organism's search for fulfillment. Openness to experience makes many more choices possible and fulfillment more likely. Unwillingness to confront the world narrows human possibilities.

3. **Feeling Threatened.** This interferes with one's freedom to move. When people feel threatened, their

perceptions narrow to concentrate on whatever seems threatening. This tunnel vision restricts the organism's search for adequacy. Threat also forces people to defend their existing positions. Both these effects are contrary to what is required for optimum growth and development.

4. **Not Caring.** People who have learned not to care are unable to make use even of the best opportunities provided for them. People attend to the things they value, so values determine the kinds of experiences people are likely to have.

5. **Having a Negative Self-concept.** People who feel inadequate become the prisoners of their own perceptions. Negative self-concepts shut people off from experience. If one does not feel able, he or she is unlikely to try. One does not try to sail a leaky vessel very far from shore.

6. **Lack of Fulfillment of Lower Level Needs.** This may prevent human beings from seeking higher level needs on what Maslow called the "hierarchy of needs." [1] With needs for food, clothing, shelter, and the basics of life unfulfilled, people are unlikely to be free to seek higher needs. It is hard to think nice thoughts about democracy on an empty belly.

Democracy and Human Motive

The basic principle of democracy, "when people are free they can find their own best ways," is essentially an affirmation of the basic human impulse to move toward fulfillment. The human organism *can* be trusted. The task of our institutions, especially the public schools, is to create the necessary conditions for freedom in which this basic drive can find expression.[2] This cannot be done if school people do not believe it is possible. Educators who do not believe that students are trustworthy can hardly be expected to let them make choices, provide them with freedom, or permit self-direction. If you don't believe people can, you don't dare let them.

FREEDOM AND LICENSE

Creating the conditions for fulfillment and health does not require letting students do as they please. Freedom is not anarchy. The factors listed earlier—knowledge, awareness, freedom from threat, caring, confidence in self, and fulfillment of one's lower level needs—do not call for license. They call for providing students with positive experience and systematically creating conditions that foster growth and development. Order, system, and law can provide the means to greater freedom for students if they are established in light of the best we know about the nature of human beings. Order, system, and law growing out of fallacious concepts about the nature of human beings, on the other hand, can inhibit and destroy the fulfillment of human potential.

Most schools have been designed and operated by persons who believed, more or less consciously, in the myth of the untrustworthy organism. As a consequence, many schools are restrictive and inhibiting institutions whose faculties and administrations are fearful of the very students they are commissioned to help. As most educators in the past have believed in the myth that the human organism can't be trusted, it comes as no surprise to find authoritarian schools, "law and order" programs, practices designed to control and direct students, motivation accomplished by complex systems of reward and punishment, and teachers behaving as though they were sitting on powder kegs likely to go off at any moment. No wonder thousands of older students cop out, drop out, or opt out of the system as soon as possible. One wonders about the little tykes, the kindergarteners and elementary school children, who do not have that option. They must live in settings incompatible with their basic natures. When people believed that the human organism was a battleground between good and evil likely to revert to basic bestiality, restricting, controlling, authoritarian schools made sense. In the light of modern knowledge about the nature of the human organism, they are no longer tolerable.

NEW ASSUMPTIONS MAKE
NEW KINDS OF SCHOOLS

Educators who begin with the assumption of a trustworthy human organism fundamentally motivated toward health and fulfillment must surely construct a very different educational system from the one just discussed. Creating conditions for human freedom is a very different goal from controlling and directing, rewarding and punishing an intransigent, contrary organism. Possessing the knowledge we now have about human nature, we cannot afford to continue basing action on the illusions of previous generations. To deny youth opportunities for maximum growth and development because we are *unwilling to create* the conditions for freedom is at least honest. To deny them opportunities because we *believe* in a myth now known to be sheer superstition is a violation of professional responsibility.

Many schools and teachers have already shifted their bases for thinking about the nature of students. Little by little they are finding effective ways for translating such understandings into educational practice. The effort is not always easy. To educators still deeply involved with the myth that the human organism can't be trusted, humanistic reforms seem "too permissive," "too progressive," or "foolhardy." Destroying a myth is a long and difficult task. It calls for courage and conviction, but the effort pays off. School systems and teachers who design policy and practice on more accurate conceptions of the nature of the persons must, necessarily, find better answers to educational questions in the long run. Their goals, techniques, and relationships will be more congruent with fact; students, in turn, will be more likely to feel their schools and teachers are relevant and rewarding.

NOTES

1. A. H. Maslow, *Motivation and Personality* (New York: Harper & Row, Publishers, 1954).
2. A. W. Combs, D. L. Avila, and W. W. Purkey, *Helping Relationships: Basic Concepts for the Helping Professions* (Boston: Allyn and Bacon, Inc., 1978).

SELECTED READINGS

Combs, A. W. *Perceiving, Behaving, Becoming* (1962 Yearbook). Washington, D.C.: Association for Supervision and Curriculum Development, 1962.

Craig, J. H., and Craig, M. *Synergic Power: Beyond Domination and Permissiveness.* Berkeley, Calif.: Pro Active Press, 1974.

Gibb, J. R., and Gibb, L. "Group Experiences and Human Possibilities." *Human Potentialities: The Challenge and the Promise.* Edited by Herbert Otto. St. Louis: Warren H. Green, Inc., 1968.

Lifton, W. W. *Working with Groups: Group Process and Individual Growth.* New York: John Wiley & Sons, Inc., 1961.

Maslow, A. H. "Synergy in the Society and the Individual." *Journal of Individual Psychology* (November 1964): 153–64.

Maslow, A. H. *The Farther Reaches of Human Nature.* New York: The Viking Press, 1971.

Rogers, C. R. *Freedom to Learn.* Columbus, Ohio: Charles E. Merrill Publishing Company, 1969.

The Myth that
They Like It That Way

A major complaint about people who seem to be out of step with the rest of us is "they like it that way." This statement is usually made in a tone of shock, frustration, disappointment, or condemnation, depending upon whether the speaker is surprised, thwarted, blaming, or rejecting. We hear it applied to nations, especially to have-not nations. We also use it to explain the failures of social experiments, as, for example, when we provide new housing for ghetto areas only to find that the residents despoil the property. We also apply it to our friends and neighbors when we do not comprehend their behavior. "How can she put up with that husband of hers? I guess she likes it that way"; or "There's no accounting for some people's taste!" The assumption is made that what people do is what they want to do. If that's so, then it follows that they deserve what happens to them.

The myth that they like it that way is not only a judgment about other people; it is also a handy excuse for inaction. If they like it that way, we really ought not interfere. We can ignore what happens to other people without feelings of guilt. For some, belief in this myth is more than an excuse for inaction. It provides an outlet for hostility and a satisfying feeling of superiority over the stupidity of other people. There are even persons for whom this myth may be a source of enjoyment, watching other people "get their just desserts." Whatever the reasons for its existence, this myth is almost totally false.

Before proceeding further with this discussion, try the following experiment which we will return to later:

DELINQUENT GANG YOUTHS' VALUES [1]

The following list of thirteen self-images was given to a large sample of individual delinquent gang youths. They were asked to rank these images in the order in which they valued them, with most valued at number 1 and least valued at number 13. See if you can rank order these images as you believe the delinquent gang youths did. Call the highest valued image number 1, the next highest valued image number 2, and so on down to number 13.

· Sticks by his friends in a fight
· Has a steady job washing and greasing cars
· Saves his money
· Is a good fighter with a tough reputation
· Knows where to sell what he steals
· Gets his kicks by using drugs
· Stays cool and keeps to himself
· Works for good grades at school
· Has good connections to avoid trouble with the law
· Likes to read good books
· Likes to spend his spare time hanging on the corner with his friends
· Makes money by pimping and other illegal hustles
· Shares his money with his friends

Save your ranking and read on.

UNDERSTANDING
HUMAN NEED

Modern psychology tells us that people do what it seems to them they must to fulfill their needs at any moment. What they do has nothing to do with liking. They may like what they do or they may hate themselves for doing it. An individual's behavior is only the best adjustment the person is able to make to the circumstances confronted at the moment of action. To recognize the truth of this statement, we need only recall some recent occasion in our own lives when we behaved in a stupid, immoral, or unsatisfactory way. At the instant of behaving, our action seemed like the best thing that could be done to satisfy our needs. The feeling we had about that sort of act before it happened, or how we would judge it afterward, was irrelevant at the moment it occurred.

People rarely misbehave because they don't know any better. Most people know what they ought to do. They behave the way it seems to them they need to at the moment of action. This is especially true for those who feel alienated, inadequate, or deprived. For such unhappy persons, their behavior represents the best defense they can muster to deal with their problems. In some mental illnesses, for example, a person who feels overwhelmed by the world may deny its existence or one who feels inadequate may decide to be someone else. Defecating in the elevator of a housing project can be a very pointed expression of hostility and anger toward the building's management or society in general. In the light of such emotions, one's taste for clean elevators is a very minor value. One of the most frequently heard complaints of the client in psychotherapy is "I know what I ought to do, but I just can't do it."

A person's behavior always represents what that person believes is necessary for personal fulfillment in the situation he or she confronts at the instant of action. It is the best solution he or she can perceive. To illustrate this point, let's return to the exercise you tried at the beginning of this chapter and compare your rankings with those actually obtained in the research. The actual findings obtained by R. A. Gordon and his colleagues in Chicago in the 1960s are reproduced in Table 1. They come from a study of two hundred and twenty-one gang youths with records showing an average of three offenses apiece. These findings were then compared with findings from another sample of lower-class and middle-class youths with few or no offenses. The data were obtained by semantic differential (a technique designed to explore personal values without asking direct questions) and were subjected to sophisticated factor analysis. The authors believe the results are accurate beyond question, pointing out that the techniques they used "ruled out all but the most ingenious and the

Table 1.   *Rank Order of Self-Images for Delinquent Gang Youths as Reported by Gordon, Short, Cartwright, and Strodtbeck*[2]

Blacks	Whites	Both	
6	5	6	Sticks by his friends in a fight
7	6	7	Has a steady job washing and greasing cars
4	3	3	Saves his money
11	9	10	Is a good fighter with a tough reputation
12	10	12	Knows where to sell what he steals
13	12	13	Gets his kicks by using drugs
5	4	5	Stays cool and keeps to himself
1	1	1	Works for good grades at school
8	8	9	Has good connections to avoid trouble with the law
3	2	2	Likes to read good books
9	7	8	Likes to spend his spare time hanging on the corner with his friends
10	11	11	Makes money by pimping and other illegal hustles
2	4	4	Shares his money with his friends

most coincidentally patterned types of deliberately meaning-less, falsified responses." [3]

Most people who have tried this exercise are astonished to discover that the gang youths' values are practically identical with those one would expect of youths in general. The behavior of these young people was not the kind of behavior they valued, but the kind possible for their personal fulfillment in the world they lived in. It is an easy thing to fall into the trap of assuming the way people behave represents what they truly like.

The Hierarchy of Needs

As mentioned in the myth that the human organism can't be trusted, Abraham Maslow described human values in a kind of hierarchy of needs from very low order needs of a physical character, like need for air, water, and food, to social needs for love and caring, to identity needs for self-esteem and achievement, to high order needs of self-actualization and fulfillment.[4] Higher order needs are almost impossible to obtain until lower ones have achieved some form of fulfillment. When lower order needs are fulfilled, people are freed to seek those at higher levels. Maladjustment is not a willful seeking of destructive or negative behavior, but a consequence of deprivation, or lack of fulfillment. The delinquent seeks maintenance and enhancement of self in those ways that seem open to him or her. To assume he or she likes it that way can only result in perpetuating his or her condition or in making it very much worse.

SOME EDUCATIONAL
CONSEQUENCES

The myth that they like it that way is especially disastrous for our public schools. Fostering the healthy growth and development of young people requires a clear understanding of the dynamics of need. Belief in this myth can only result in the following:

1. **Strained Communication Between Teachers, Students, and Administrators.** False assumptions about other people's motives are bound to result in confusion and misunderstanding. This contributes further to the generation gap and the feeling, already held by too many youths, that school is irrelevant.

2. **Rejection of Those Students Most in Need of Help and Understanding.** Maslow described the behaviors of the maladjusted as "the screams of the tortured at the crushing of their psychological bones."[5] Turning a deaf ear to such screams, in a mistaken belief in the myth that they like it that way, denies young people the aid and assistance public schools have been created to provide.

3. **Failure to Diagnose What Really Needs to be Done.** Action plans based on false assumptions can only result in inadequate programs and the perpetuation or exacerbation of problems. Clear understanding of the dynamics of need, on the other hand, provides firm bases from which to examine problems and arrive at more adequate solutions.

In this and the previous chapter, we have seen that modern psychology postulates a basic human need to move toward health if the way is open to do so. This means that students and teachers want the same thing—for students to become the best they can be. Full realization of this fact makes a great difference in the kinds of schools, practices, objectives, and human relationships we attempt to construct. How we behave toward people we think are against us is bound to be different from how we act toward those we regard as on our side. Building educational systems on this premise should make our schools not only more efficient, but more humane, happier places for students to live and teachers to work.

NOTES

1. Adapted from R. A. Gordon, J. F. Short, D. S. Cartwright and F. L. Strodtbeck, "Group Process and Gang Delinquency," *American Journal of Sociology* 69 (September 1963): 109–28. Copyright 1963 by the University of Chicago.
2. Ibid.
3. Ibid.
4. A. H. Maslow, *Motivation and Personality* (New York: Harper & Row, Publishers, 1954).
5. As described by A. H. Maslow in a speech given in Gainesville, Florida in 1961.

SELECTED READINGS

Erikson, E. *Identity: Youth and Crisis.* New York: W. W. Norton & Company, Inc., 1969.

Fair, C. M. "The Reluctant Student: Perspectives on Feeling States and Motivation." *Feeling, Valuing and the Art of Growing* (1977 Yearbook). Washington, D.C.: Association for Supervision and Curriculum Development, 1977.

Frankl, V. *Man's Search for Meaning.* New York: Washington Square Press, 1963.

Harrington, M. *The Other America.* Baltimore, Md.: Penguin Books, 1963.

Maslow, A. "Our Maligned Human Nature." *Journal of Psychology* 28 (1949): 273–78.

Orem, R. C. *Montessori Today.* New York: G. P. Putnam's Sons, 1971.

The Myth of Fixed Intelligence

For many generations, educators and members of the general public have labored under the illusion that human intelligence is fixed and immutable. Intelligence, it has been believed, is the inborn, ultimate limit of one's capacities. Parents and teachers could help a child fulfill that destiny, but limits could never be exceeded. This very old myth had its roots in the ancient idea that human characteristics were permanently established by God. It was further corroborated by observations open to anyone that people do, indeed, behave in ways that are bright or stupid. Since intelligent parents often have brighter children and dull parents seem to have slower offspring, people concluded that differences in intelligence are absolutely set by heredity. This myth is still at work in recent times; a number of psychologists have even given it the stamp of scientific fact.

SOME EFFECTS ON SCHOOLS

This unfortunate myth has worked its sinister consequences on generations of public school children. In its name, children have been classified as *gifted, average, dull, educationally mentally retarded,* or *mentally retarded* and grouped or tracked accordingly because "it is more efficient to treat children according to their established ability levels." Test makers and sellers have grown rich on the profits from intelligence tests. Children's IQ's have often been accorded the sacrosanct character of doctors' prescriptions. Teachers have seen themselves as the victims of the child's intelligence, and their goals as strictly limited by the student's innate potential. For many years, nobody raised a question about this because everyone knew "that intelligence is what people are born with."

PEOPLE ARE OVERBUILT

Many contemporary psychologists take a quite different view of intelligence. They point out that the outstanding characteristic of human beings is, not their limitations, but their possibilities.[1] Each of us, they tell us, is overbuilt. When an architect designs a building, he builds into it a strength and safety factor far greater than he ever expects the building to require. Human beings are like that too. Each of us has potentialities far in excess of what we are ever called upon to use. This, of course, is the way it had to be. If human beings had not had the potential to rise to crisis occasions, they would not have made it through the chain of evolution. No matter what potential we are born with, none of us ever achieves more than the smallest fraction of what we might be.

BEHAVIOR TRANSCENDS
THE ORGANISM

We are accustomed to thinking of human limits in physical terms. We know that when we are ill we can't run so fast, and when we are old we can't climb so well, and when we are handicapped we can't perform as we would like. These physical limits on our behavior are real and compelling. But most of the behavior required to live and work intelligently in modern society is only minimally physical.

How intelligently we behave is primarily a question of our beliefs, understandings, values, feelings, emotions, wants, loves, hates, fears, desires, and aspirations. These are the *causes* of our behavior. These causes take place in a physical body, but given a reasonably healthy one, people are no longer restricted by the structure of the body itself. To draw an analogy, the structure of an automobile sets rough limits on its behavior. It cannot go far under water or in the air. If it is in working order, however, where it can go on land is no longer determined by its mechanical makeup.

The capacity for intelligent behavior is only in small degree a physical function. It is far more a consequence of a person's perceptual field. That is to say, how intelligently a person can behave is a function of the richness, extent, and availability of his or her personal experience. This experience, of course, is in part dependent on the physical organism. For example, it is necessary to have eyes to see. Given eyes that see, however, what one sees, what one has seen, and what one will see in the future is no longer a question of body structure.

Some Factors Determining Intelligence

Given a reasonable state of health, the richness, extent, and availability of experience will be dependent upon at least the following factors. All of these factors are open to change or manipulation.

1. **Time.** Generally speaking, the longer a person lives and is exposed to life, the more experience he or she acquires.

2. **The Environment.** The kinds of environments people live in have inevitable effects upon their experience. Eskimos, for example, do not comprehend bananas, nor natives of the Amazon, snow.

3. **The Effect of Need.**   People perceive what they need to perceive. When looking for a friend's house on a street we've driven a hundred times, we may see many things we have often passed without noticing.

4. **The Self-concept.**   People behave in terms of what they believe about themselves. Whether we feel adequate or inadequate greatly affects how we approach a task.

5. **Values.**   People perceive what they value either positively or negatively. Little girls see horses quite differently than their fathers. Herpetologists view snakes very differently from the average man on the street.

6. **Challenge and Threat.**   People perceive events they view as threatening quite differently from events they view as enhancing.

CAN INTELLIGENCE REALLY BE CHANGED?

The idea that intelligence is subject to change is one of the most exciting in modern psychology. Today we are being told by the most respected authorities that intelligence can be changed much more than we ever previously believed possible. Recent data, for example, have shown that intelligence levels of children and adults can improve considerably as a consequence of enriched experience. Deprivation, on the other hand, accompanies falling levels of performance.[2] After reviewing the research on changing intelligence, psychologist J. McV. Hunt concluded:

It is highly unlikely that any society has developed a system of child rearing and education that maximizes the potential of the individuals which compose it. Probably no individual has ever lived whose full potential for happy intellectual interest and growth has been achieved. Various bits of the evidence reviewed hint that if the manner in which encounters with the environment foster the development of intellectual interest and capacity were more fully understood, it might be possible to increase the average level of intelligence within the population substantially. The hope of increasing the average level of intelligence by proper manipulation of children's developmental encounters with their environments, a hope which becomes reasonable with the evidences surveyed here and with relinquishing the assumptions of fixed intelligence and predetermined development, provides a challenge of the first order.[3]

Alfred Binet, the father of intelligence testing, also supported the concept of changing intelligence. In fact, he probably would have been deeply distressed at the uses we have made of his tests. In 1909 he wrote:

Some recent philosophers appear to have given their support to the deplorable verdict that intelligence of an individual is a fixed quantity, a quantity which cannot be augmented. We must protest and act against this brutal pessimism. . . .

A child's mind is like a field in which an expert farmer has advised a change in the method of cultivation with the result that in place of desert land we now have a harvest. It is in this particular sense, the only one which is significant, that we say that the intelligence of children may be increased. One increases that which constitutes the intelligence of a school child, namely, the capacity to learn, to improve with instruction.[4]

What a pity we did not pay closer attention to his admonition. For years we have lived with the myth of fixed intelligence. Blinded by our former conceptions about human capacity, we made little effort to change the status quo.

For additional references bearing on the question of changing intelligence, see the Selected Readings at the end of this chapter.

CREATING INTELLIGENCE—NEW GOALS FOR EDUCATION

Modern ideas about intelligence tell us that human capacity can be created. Teachers and parents are not merely the victims of a child's hereditary capacity; they are important factors in producing it. Imagine, for example, what could be done by using factors affecting intelligence that were outlined earlier—time, environment, effect of need, self-concept, values, and challenge and threat. What might be done, for example, if we were to systematically improve the physical condition of all youths? What kinds of environments could we construct that might more effectively result in enriched perceptions for children? What possible effects might occur from a systematic attempt to provide real satisfaction for children's most pressing needs? What would happen if we were to consciously and carefully provide experiences that would lead people to conceptions of themselves as able, worthy, acceptable, loved, and wanted? What might be done in our public schools to assist our youth in the exploration and discovery of values? Finally, what kind of society might we produce if we were honestly to set ourselves the task of designing experiences to challenge children without threatening them?

We have lived with the myth of fixed intelligence a very long time. It was a dreary, dull concept at best. It has stymied our efforts to raise the level of education and has committed us to the continuation of the status quo for generations. The damage it has done to millions of children must surely have been stupendous. We are fortunate that we can now discard this myth and base our actions on concepts more positive, hopeful, and fulfilling. So fundamental a shift in our thinking about the nature of human beings has implications for every aspect of our society, but especially for schools whose primary goal is the nurturance of intelligent behavior.

It's true that we are still a long way from knowing how to go about improving human intelligence on a grand scale. Even so, knowing it can be improved is very much better than thinking it cannot be done. A defeatist attitude is self-fulfilling. People will try what seems to them to be possible; our new understandings are pointing the way to areas we can explore to find new and better ways to increase the capacities of youth for more intelligent behavior. Now that we know it is possible to create intelligence, we must get about the business of doing it whenever and wherever possible. One way to begin is to systematically apply the questions we have asked here to the curriculum and practices of public education at every level.

NOTES

1. A. W. Combs, "Intelligence from a Perceptual Point of View," *Journal of Abnormal and Social Psychology* 47 (1952): 662–673.

2. I. J. Gordon, "A Parent Education Approach to Provision of Early Stimulation for the Culturally Disadvantaged," A final report for the Ford Foundation (Gainesville, Florida: Institute for the Development of Human Resources, 1967).

3. J. McV. Hunt, *Intelligence and Experience.* Copyright © 1961, The Ronald Press Company, New York, p. 346.

4. Alfred Binet, *Les Idees Modernes sur les Enfants* (Paris: Ernest Flamarion, 1909), pp. 54–55.

SELECTED READINGS

Combs, A. W. "Intelligence from a Perceptual Point of View." *Journal of Abnormal and Social Psychology* 47 (1952): 662–73.

Combs, A. W., Richards, A. C., and Richards, F. *Perceptual Psychology: A Humanistic View of the Psychology of Persons.* New York: Harper & Row, Publishers, 1976.

Gordon, I. J. *Early Child Stimulation Through Parent Education.* University of Florida Institute for the Development of Human Resources. Final report to the Children's Bureau, Department of Health, Education and Welfare, Washington, D.C., 1969.

Hunt, J. McV. *Human Intelligence.* New Brunswick, N.J.: Transaction, Inc., 1970.

Maslow, A. *The Farther Reaches of Human Nature.* New York: The Viking Press, 1971.

Ornstein, R. *The Psychology of Consciousness.* San Francisco: W. H. Freeman and Company, Publishers, 1972.

Otto, H. A. *Human Potentialities: The Challenge and the Promise.* St. Louis: Warren H. Green, Inc., 1968.

Ouspensky, P. D. *The Psychology of Man's Possible Evolution.* New York: Bantam Books, Inc., 1968.

The Myth of
the Neglected Gifted Child

A frequent complaint about public schools is that they are organized for the average child and as a consequence, gifted children are frightfully neglected. Gifted children, the complaint continues, need to be identified early, to be given special attention, and to be stimulated toward the maximum fulfillment of their magnificent potential. An accompanying grievance is that we spend an unwarranted amount of money on average and handicapped children while investing a vastly smaller amount in gifted children who are the promise of the future. As usual, there is a germ of truth in this myth. A few gifted children are, indeed, victims of neglect in our public schools. Most gifted children, however, are vastly better off than their average or handicapped peers. The fact is, we do not do nearly enough for *any* child in our public schools. Out of that inadequate effort, gifted children get more than their share.

THE GENERALLY-NEGLECTED
MYTH

Some people feel that gifted children are generally neglected in the classroom. This is a myth that could not have been expounded by anyone who knew very much about American schools. Far from being neglected, gifted children are likely to be the petted and pampered darlings of the teachers they encounter. Teachers will fight tooth and nail to teach the "gifted sections" or have a gifted child assigned to their class. They fight just as hard to avoid assignment to "average," "slow," or "retarded" sections. Teaching the so-called brighter students is a mark of prestige and status in the teachers' lounge. It is also regarded as a special plum by the administration to be awarded to the very best teachers. This assignment of teachers follows exactly the opposite principle from that used in most other professions. The medical profession, for example, assigns its very best doctors and surgeons to the most difficult, intransigent cases. In education, we make a practice of assigning our best teachers to the children who need them least. In the case of the gifted, the best teachers are assigned to those who would learn whether a teacher was assigned to them or not.

Gifted children in the classroom are seldom truly neglected. Quite the contrary, they are likely to be the "stars" of the room. Because of their obvious success, everyone quickly classifies them as "smart" and bows to their superior ability. Because they do things so well, they are continually upheld as models for others to emulate and they are likely to be trotted out on every occasion when the teacher desires to impress the administration or visitors. Because they finish work sooner, gifted children get to do more extra things, and have more special privileges and more freedom from ordinary constraints. All this can only contribute to making them more special than ever. Like the old saying, "the rich get richer and the poor get poorer." Under such treatment some gifted children may also develop insufferable egos.

THE NEED FOR
STIMULATION MYTH

The myth that gifted children need to be identified and specially stimulated is equally questionable. The fundamental bases of intelligence, we now understand, are established as a consequence of early stimulation. Gifted children are thus already products of successful stimulation. Because of their broader, richer stores of perceptions, they also have, at any moment, far greater possibilities for generating their own further development. As a consequence, they are likely to be more motivated, more curious, and more open to further experience than most of their lesser-favored peers. Left to their own devices, they are far more capable of finding things to do. To be sure, they may not direct their energies to explorations approved by their teachers, but surely they are not in need of being pushed and prodded.

Anyone who has ever had the experience of raising a truly gifted child can attest to the fact that gifted children do not ordinarily need to be further stimulated. Quite the contrary, the greater need is to protect them from exploitation. Truly gifted children are so much the center of attention that they are continually being asked or required to behave in exemplary ways. Because of their unique abilities, they spring at once to the attention of teachers and administrators whenever special things are to be done. "Who shall we get to write the class poem?" "Susie, she does it so well." "Who shall we send to the Youth Conference to represent our school?" "Susie would do a great job." "Who shall we get to make a speech for our class?" "Susie, she speaks so well." "Who shall we get to make a poster, go to the library, run for office?" "Susie, she does it so well." Most gifted children have their days packed from end to end with stimulation and expectations, if not from within themselves, then from others around them. Gifted kids are self-starters. With freedom and opportunity, their inner wellsprings will provide the motivation for exploration and growth. Outside attempts to funnel or channel their interests into particular directions may result in squelching the very initiative and creativity they have in such precious supply.

THE FINANCIAL NEGLECT MYTH

Closely related to the belief that gifted children are badly neglected in our public schools is the allegation that we are not spending enough money on them. Gifted children are simply not getting their fair share of the tax dollar, says the complaint. As a matter of fact, we probably spend more money on gifted children than on any other group in our entire school system. If that statement sounds shocking, we need only remind ourselves of the money we spend for colleges and universities, assistantships, scholarships, teaching grants, research subsidies, and the like. All these are intended for the brightest students and add up to a very large figure. The fact is, we do not spend enough on educating *any* student. Of the total sum we do spend, the best students receive a very fair share.

CHANGING OUR ATTITUDE

In the discussion of the myth of fixed intelligence, we saw that modern psychologists now believe intelligence to be a function of experience and can therefore be created (*see* page 105). If this is true, an entirely different view of giftedness is called for. When we believed intelligence was something people were born with, it made sense to regard gifted children as very special persons to be identified early and thereafter nurtured and stimulated. That way they might fulfill the leadership roles destined by their genetics. Now that we know people are not *born* gifted, but *become* gifted as a consequence of their experiences in growing up, we need to change our attitude so as to create the kind of environments likely to produce such children in much larger numbers.

Gifted children are our crowning achievements. They are the children with whom we have already been extraordinarily successful. But, we did not intentionally produce them, so the pressing task before us is to find out how we did it. Once we know that, we can get about the business of creating many more gifted children in the future. Who knows what kind of society we might be able to develop through conscious, purposeful attempts to provide all children the good things we have given the gifted by chance? The world is sorely in need of all the intelligent people we can grow. The effort to discover ways to develop giftedness is long overdue.

SELECTED READINGS

Ausubel, D. P. "The Prestige Motivation of Gifted Children." *Genetic Psychology Monograph* 42 (1952): 53–117.

Barrett, H. O. "An Intensive Study of 32 Gifted Children." *Personnel and Guidance Journal* 36 (1957): 192–94.

Getzels, J. W., and Jackson, P. W. *Creativity and Intelligence: Explorations with Gifted Students.* New York: John Wiley & Sons, Inc., 1962.

Smidchens, V., and Sellin, D. "Attitudes toward Mentally Gifted Learners." *Gifted Child Quarterly* 20 (1976): 109–13.

The Myth of the Value of Failure

One of the most pernicious myths in education is the myth of the value of failure. Millions believe that failure is good for people, that experiencing failure is somehow strengthening and ennobling. So widespread is this myth in our society that failure is not only condoned in our public schools but strenuously advocated. The use of competition, grade level organization, promotion, and all sorts of devices to reward and punish, for example, is widely advocated as valuable for motivating students.

In fact, failure is essentially destructive to human personality and achievement. Psychologists tell us that failure, psychologically, is like disease physiologically. Disease is a consequence of interference with the body's growth and development; similarly, failure represents interference with the growth of a person. We do not believe that diseases are good for us. We do not say about them, "Let's give this child all the diseases we can as soon as possible." Rather, we say, "Let's keep this child from contracting disease as long as we possibly can." Or, alternatively we say, "Let's give this child the disease in such a weakened form that we know he or she will have a success experience with it." We protect our children against physical disease by giving them success experiences in the form of inoculations, immunizations, vaccinations, and the like, knowing that successful experiences with attenuated forms of disease will contribute to the possibilities of dealing with the real thing when it comes along later. We should be treating academic and psychological failure the same way we treat disease; they are equally destructive. How differently we deal with failure.

THE NATURE OF FAILURE

In our society, not succeeding is more than just a fact, it is an indication of personal inferiority. Affixing this judgment is something that must be learned. Children do not understand the concept of failure until 'they are taught. But they are taught very early, even before they come to school. For example, watching a child playing with blocks, I may say to him, "Eddie, that's a nice house you're building." He turns to me with pleasure and says, "Yeah," and then points to his friend saying: "Jimmy's a good house builder, too. Jimmy's a gooder house builder than me." He is happy for himself and happy for his friend, Jimmy, too—until some interfering adult enters the picture to ask: "And what's the matter with you, son? How come you don't build as good a house as Jimmy?" So an experience of joy and accomplishment is turned into a lesson in competition and degradation. Nonachievement of goals, which should be no more than a factual observation, is changed into a matter of personal evaluation and humiliation.

What makes a failure is not the fact of nonaccomplishment, but the value judgment attached to the observation. The invidious, degrading connotation of failure is hammered home thousands of times in a child's public school experience. In fact, the myth of the value of failure is so widespread, we do not even have an appropriate word to express the idea that a person attempted something that did not succeed except the word *failure*. What's more, the word *failure* is in itself a value judgment. It always carries with it the connotation that the failer is a culprit, or an obnoxious or repugnant individual. Mistakes or experiments in living that didn't pan out are not treated as sources of valuable data from which good things can be learned. They are labeled *FAILURES* and are accompanied by shame and degradation. Worse still, experiencing failure is widely acclaimed for its positive contributions to personal growth and development.

FAILURE AND SUCCESS

Failure is debilitating and destructive to human beings. Success, on the other hand, is strengthening and sustaining. The best guarantee that a person will be successful in the future is that he or she has been successful in the past. Contemporary studies of supremely healthy, self-actualizing, well-adjusted persons have shown that experiences of success provide strength and security. A major characteristic of such people is feeling positively about themselves. They see themselves as persons who are liked, wanted, successful, and able. Possessing such feelings provides them with an inner core of security that makes it possible to behave much more effectively in dealing with all aspects of life. The person with positive feelings about himself or herself has a firm base from which to deal more successfully with the exigencies of life as they occur. With a stout ship under one's feet it is possible to sail far from shore. When one has grave doubts about his ship, sailing is much more hazardous and one dares not go very far from safe harbor.

Positive views of self are learned. They are learned by experiencing success, not failure. Even the "self-made man," who proudly points to himself as a product of struggle and the ennobling qualities of hard knocks, is, himself, a walking exhibit of the value of success. His accomplishments are not proof of the value of failure; quite the contrary. He became the self-made man he is on a diet of success. Had he not been successful, he would not have become a self-made man. As pointed out in the myth that if it's hard it's good for you, people grow through confronting problems when they are successful in handling them. Even nonsuccess with problems can be constructive if the experience is perceived merely as a source of data to be used for what it is worth in guiding future action. What destroys the value of problem-solving experience is labeling it *failure* with all the connotations of personal inadequacy, guilt, and degradation that accompany that word. Labeling an experience *failure* converts a valuable human experience into a debilitating, hindering one.

The core of personal security provided by a diet of success makes it possible for people to be far more creative. Creativity is a consequence of being different, of daring to try, of venturing into the new and unknown. Like sailing the ship in the earlier analogy, such explorations are far more possible and likely for persons with the security of a positive self-concept. An inner core of security also permits the possessor to be more open to experience than people without such confidence in themselves. Confident persons can approach life more gladly, joyfully, and openly without needing to surround themselves with self-contrived fences as protection against the outside world. Such openness to experience is also characteristic of more intelligent human beings. People more open to experience have much more data from which to make their choices. This means better answers to problems and that is what intelligence is all about.

EDUCATION WITHOUT FAILURE

In light of contemporary knowledge about the effects of failure on the human personality, there would seem to be no place for such experience in our public schools. Yet, failure can be observed everywhere in the system. Despite all the evidence supporting the negative effects of failure, it is still stoutly advocated as a valuable motivation for learning. The myth is so deeply ingrained that its insidious influence pervades every aspect of our schools at every level. Even when teachers and administrators understand and deplore the effects of failure, and honestly seek to operate in nonthreatening ways, its negative consequences persist in the experience of students. What makes an event a *failure* is not what the teacher thinks is happening but what the student is experiencing. So, many a well-laid plan for encouraging and motivating students may run aground because students perceive it as humiliating or discouraging. Programs designed to eliminate failure must be constructed from the point of view of the student if they are to be truly effective.

Only a major effort to eliminate the insidious effects of failure is likely to have much impact on our educational system. Even then, it will probably take several generations before much headway can be achieved. No matter how difficult it may be, the effort must be made. It is unthinkable that education should continue to ignore the effects of failure so clearly indicated by modern psychological science.

The goal of education is to prepare youth to deal successfully with problems both now and in the future. If it is true that successful experiences are the best preparation for achieving future success, then schools must find ways of helping each student experience success in the course of his or her schooling.[1] The first step toward that end must be a proper appreciation of the mythical character of the value of failure and its destructive effects upon human beings. One shudders to think of the staggering losses in human potential the world has already suffered because of the belief in the value of failure. The sooner we dispense with its cancerous effects upon our thinking, the sooner we can get about the business of creating the kinds of schools our society needs and our young people deserve.

NOTE

1. William Glasser, *Schools Without Failure* (New York: Harper & Row, Publishers, 1969).

SELECTED READINGS

Coopersmith, S. *The Antecedents of Self-Esteem.* San Francisco: W. H. Freeman and Company, Publishers, 1967.

Coudert, J. *Advice from a Failure.* New York: Dell Publishing Co., Inc., 1965.

Diller, L. "Conscious and Unconscious Self-attitudes After Success and Failure." *Journal of Personality* 23 (1954): 1–12.

Fitts, W. H. "The Self-concept and Behavior: Overview and Supplement." Nashville: Dede Wallace Center, 1972.

Glasser, W. *Schools Without Failure.* New York: Harper & Row, Publishers, 1969.

Holt, J. C. *How Children Fail.* New York: Pitman Publishing Corporation, 1964.

Skinner, B. F. *Science and Human Behavior.* New York: Macmillan, Inc., 1953.

The Myth of
the Value of Punishment

Further extensions of the law and order myth we discussed earlier are the myth of the value of punishment as a motivator in education and its allied myth that there's nothing a good flogging won't ordinarily cure. As far back in time as we can observe, people have used various forms of punishment to control the behavior of others. Education, however, cannot be satisfied to merely control behavior; schools are for learning. Everything done in schools must contribute to the learning process. This goes for punishment, too. If it is to be employed, then schools need the clearest possible understanding of its assets and liabilities so as to determine what uses can be made of it.

In examining punishment, we need to differentiate between punishment in a physical context and punishment in a social context. For example, a child might be punished by a hot stove (physical) or by an angry parent (social).[1] In the physical context, when a child touches a hot stove the punishment is usually no more involved than some slightly burned fingers. This is an objective, unemotional encounter with life. The causes and consequences are clear to everyone. A person, unless very ill, can't remain angry at or hold a grudge against a stove for long, and he or she certainly can't gain much satisfaction by taking revenge on the punisher. Punishment inflicted by one human being on another in a social context is something else. When an angry parent punishes his or her child for being disobedient, much subjectivity and emotion are involved. What the child experiences may be very different from what the parent intended and what the child learned from the experience may be a far cry from parental expectations. The unpredictable character of the effects of punishment in a social context makes its value for learning highly questionable.

THE USES OF PUNISHMENT

Punishment as a means for controlling behavior is essentially a management technique, a device for controlling people through the manipulation of external forces. In the light of contemporary psychological understanding, the value of punishment is highly limited. Its contribution to the process of learning lies in three general areas: (1) Punishment teaches people what *not* to do; (2) Punishment teaches highly specific behaviors; and (3) Punishment's effects are temporary.

Teaching What Not to Do

People rarely learn what to do through punishment—only what not to do. Punishment is essentially a negative technique. Its teaching value lies primarily in stopping or diverting a particular behavior. A child may be taught not to play in the street by whacking his bottom when he steps off the curb. Teaching him how and when and where to cross streets safely requires instruction in many broader factors such as the priority rights of cars, trucks, and people; proper places for crossing; the problems of driver vision and of stopping vehicles quickly; and even matters of custom and courtesy. Most human behaviors are far more complex than they appear on the surface. Learning to behave effectively is an involved process of exploration and personal discovery in which punishment plays but a very small part.

Teaching Highly Specific Behaviors

The effects of punishment are highly specific. Its value is strictly limited to the precise act being punished. The use of punishment for teaching broader concepts is very discouraging. In our family we have two cats which are forbidden to go upstairs to our bedrooms. By conscientiously punishing them whenever they set foot on the stairs, we thoroughly taught them not to go upstairs—when we are at home! We know from the evidence of footprints across the bedspread, plants knocked off the window ledge, and cat hairs on a chair seat that when we are away our carefully taught prohibitions do not deter our cats. If we come in quietly, we can often surprise them rushing pell mell downstairs where they know they belong—when we are there. The effect of punishment is like that. After one has taught a student not to perform in a disapproved fashion, there are still numerous behaviors from which he or she can make further choices. If the only device we have for helping a student learn what to do is punishment, schooling becomes a grim and forbidding business, seeking to block off each wrong answer as it appears. Punishment is a precision tool applicable to highly specific purposes.

Punishment's Temporary Effect

The effects of punishment are usually temporary, especially when it has been used to block strongly desired behavior. When desire is strong and continuous, punishment or the threat of punishment must also be continuous. As B. F. Skinner suggests: "The benefits of punishment are temporary, and there are often unwanted and long-lasting by-products. We live in a very punishment-oriented world, partly because it is easier and quicker to punish than to take the time to handle a situation positively." [2] It is a basic principle of conditioning that the conditioned response tends to extinguish if it is not reinforced from time to time. Because punishment is primarily a deterrent, the punishing behavior must be kept in place, either really or symbolically, if its effects are to be long-term. Punishing to control behavior is like building a dam to hold back the waters of a creek. The waters can be contained only so long as the dam remains in place.

SIDE EFFECTS OF PUNISHMENT

As we have seen repeatedly in this book, the germ of truth inherent in many myths is diluted or destroyed by the side effects that accompany its application. This is true for the effects of punishment. Even the limited contributions we have just explored may be negated in the larger perspective by at least three very important side effects: (1) Punishment is experienced by the recipient as a form of threat; (2) Punishment often generates negative responses; and (3) Punishment spreads from the behavior to the behaver.

Punishment Is Experienced by the Recipient as a Form of Threat

The purpose of education is to open one to experience, to expand awareness, and to contribute to the development of an ever more adequate self. The effects of threat, in narrowing perception and forcing defense of self, are directly contrary to those objectives. Schools must challenge students, not threaten them. Punishment is rarely challenging and nearly always threatening. In fact, it is the threatening quality of punishment that makes it useful for the limited effects pointed out earlier.

Punishment Often Generates
Negative Responses

Persons who are punished become fearful, anxious, and hostile. They often retaliate for the pain and embarrassment they have suffered by striking out at others. Under such conditions, it is doubtful that any good thing is likely to be learned. Punishment is a vengeful kind of human response, usually made in the heat of anger and frustrated emotions. The results are seldom any better for the administrator of the punishment than for the recipient. Even worse, punishment often has a circular effect. The more a person is punished, the more frustrated and hostile he or she becomes. This causes that person to strike back even more forcefully, thereby causing the punisher to become more frustrated and angry and to punish harder and with greater furor than before. As B. F. Skinner points out: "Punishment usually doesn't work in the absence of the punisher. If it does, chances are the motivation is a well-developed guilt complex that does a lot of damage to what people call personality. The by-products of punishment are conflict, aggressiveness, deception, revenge—emotional problems that account for many hangups in later life." [3] Such negative consequences of using punishment cannot be ignored in the classroom. To do so may only frustrate the objectives of education and destroy what ought to be positive growth experience.

Punishment Spreads from the Behavior
to the Behaver

It is easy for a child to mistake "badness" in self for badness in the act that is being punished. It is a simple jump to believe that it is *me*, not my behavior, that is bad. This is an aspect of punishment too important to be ignored. In view of what psychologists now understand about the self-concept and its importance in every aspect of human behavior, whatever contributes to the erosion of a positive self-concept or to the building of a negative one must be evaluated with great care. With the best of intentions, punishment directed at stopping a particular behavior may be easily translated by the student into a personal evaluation of self. This can happen with almost any kind of punishment, but often the effect is not accidental. The administrator of the punishment may consciously use negative evaluation of self as an additional punishment device. For example, a teacher may say: "If you don't stop that, Jimmy, you will have to change your seat. You want to be a good boy, don't you?" So punishment is not just intended to inhibit a disapproved behavior. The demeaning effect on self is consciously and intentionally used as a means of control. What began as correction of a simple misbehavior becomes a moral, personal issue. The child is not only punished for the act he or she performed, the value of his or her self is brought into question.

Society needs a disciplined citizenry. A disciplined citizen, however, is not synonymous with a punished citizen. Discipline is a consequence of fundamental beliefs about self and others, about human rights and responsibilities, and about cooperative effort and willingness to carry one's full share in an interacting world. These are internal values acquired through personal experience and discovery. They cannot be taught by punishment. In fact, excessive punishment will almost certainly result in just the opposite beliefs.

The use of punishment for controlling misbehavior in school is at times inevitable. Sometimes, the consequences of an act a person is **about to** perform are so dire that there may be no time for another alternative. Sometimes, it may be required to manage obstreperous behavior. As a tool for teaching, however, punishment generally leaves much to be desired. While it may on occasion be necessary to employ it, teachers need to be fully aware of the dynamics involved in its use, especially with the side effects it produces in the student. Without an awareness of these, the use of punishment may result in destroying with the left hand what the right hand is attempting to accomplish. Education must be much more than management. The goal of education is the production of intelligent behavior—the production of autonomous, independent, self-directing, responsible, problem-solving, forever-seeking persons. These are general, global characteristics. They are internal matters achieved by deeply personal exploration and discovery. They are nurtured most surely by others who are helping, facilitating persons with a deep respect for the dignity and integrity of all people. Punishment has been the favored instrument of tyrants, dictators, and authoritarians throughout human history. Its place must surely be rare in the kind of schools we need in a free, democratic society.

NOTES

1. Portions of this discussion are based on a section on punishment in: A. W. Combs, D. L. Avila and W. W. Purkey, *Helping Relationships: Basic Concepts for the Helping Professions* (Boston: Allyn and Bacon, Inc., 1978).
2. M. Wilhelm, "Ideas for Living No. 16—Interview with B. F. Skinner," *Family Circle* 87 (October 1975): 8ff.
3. Ibid.

SELECTED READINGS

Abramson, P. "Discipline: Not the Worst Problem . . . But Bad. *Grade Teacher* 86 (1968): 151–63.

Avila, D. L., and Purkey, W. W. "Intrinsic and Extrinsic Motivation: A Regrettable Distinction." *Psychology in the Schools* 3 (1966): 206–08.

Kounin, J. S., and Gump, P. V. "Ripple Effect in Discipline." *Elementary School Journal* 59 (1958): 158–62.

Logan, F. A., and Wagner, A. R. *Reward and Punishment*. Boston: Allyn and Bacon, Inc., 1965.

Mallios, H. C. "Corporal Punishment and the Law: The Eighth Amendment." *High School Journal* 59 (1976): 182–91.

Marshall, H. H. "The Effect of Punishment of Children: A Review of the Literature and a Suggested Hypothesis." *Journal of Genetic Psychology* 106 (1965): 23–33.

Webster, S. W. *Discipline in the Classroom*. San Francisco: Chandler, 1968.

The Myth of Irresponsible Youth

A common complaint about modern youth is that they are irresponsible. These criticisms often arise because young people have refused to accept the values esteemed by their elders. But rejecting the values of a former generation has nothing to do with responsibility or the lack of it. If there is a germ of truth in the complaint that many young people seem less responsible than others would like them to be, and there is, it's more an indictment of our schools than a comment on the nature of youth. Responsibility and irresponsibility are not inborn characteristics. They are traits learned in the process of growing up. A major function of schools is to develop responsible citizens. If youth are truly irresponsible, schools must accept some of the blame.

RESPONSIBILITY IS LEARNED

Responsibility is learned, like any other subject, through experience. We learn to be responsible through success experiences, first with simple tasks and then with increasingly larger, more difficult tasks as our capacity increases. Responsibility is learned from *being given* responsibility; it is never learned from having it withheld. For example, the elementary teacher, who leaves her class on their own and returns to find them disorderly, may express her annoyance and disappointment by telling the class "I will never leave you alone again." By such a decision she robs those children of their only opportunity to learn how to behave when a teacher is not there. They cannot learn how to behave when the teacher is not there if the teacher never leaves them. We can only learn responsibility by having opportunities to try our wings and develop our skills. In this way we will acquire the confidence to deal with larger and larger issues. Just like learning to add and subtract, to read, and to recognize geography, we learn to deal with more difficult tasks by successfully completing simpler ones.

While responsibility is almost certain to rank high on any list of educational objectives, it rarely finds specific expression in school curricula. It is a fascinating thing that kindergarten children, who are presumably less able to make decisions than older children, make hundreds of choices about all kinds of matters in the course of a day. But the farther up the educational ladder a child progresses, presumably with increasing capacity, the fewer decisions he or she is permitted to make. Learning to be responsible requires being allowed to make decisions, to observe results, and to deal with the consequences of those decisions. A curriculum designed to teach responsibility needs to provide continuous opportunities for students to engage in such processes. To do so, however, requires taking risks, a terribly frightening prospect for many teachers and administrators.

THE PARALYZING EFFECTS OF
THE FEAR OF MAKING MISTAKES

Education is built on right answers. Students are graded on their ability to provide the correct answers and are blamed and punished for having wrong ones. This preoccupation with being right so pervades our educational system that everyone, from top to bottom, becomes fearful of making mistakes. This, in turn, has disastrous consequences on the production of responsibility.

Fear of making mistakes results in maintaining the status quo. Nothing can be done for fear of the risks involved. Everyone seeks to cover himself or herself against any possible criticism. Playing it safe becomes the order of the day. Field trips are discouraged for fear of "what might happen." Experiments are avoided for fear of criticism. Subjects are not dealt with because parents may object. Judgments are not made unless they can be carefully documented at every step. The fear of making mistakes pervades and immobilizes the educational system at every level. Teachers and students, afraid to try, are condemned to spend their days doing and redoing the expected. This can only result in the dullest, most dismal curricular experiences for everyone, teachers and students alike.

Horrible examples of what happens when schools are afraid to let students make mistakes can be seen in the standard farce of student government. The game goes something like this: Students are encouraged to form a government. They do so and proceed to pass a law. The law, however, is vetoed by the administration and the students are told they cannot do that. The government tries again and once again its efforts are vetoed. Students are not stupid. They quickly get the message. Their student government is not for real; it's only pretend. Having come to this conclusion, they proceed to treat it as a joke. This horrifies the faculty who exclaim in high dudgeon: "Look at that! They don't even treat their own student government seriously!" So, loudly proclaiming the lack of responsibility on the part of the students, the faculty fails to recognize its own responsibility in bringing about that state of affairs.

Teaching Responsibility Requires
Taking Risks

A program productive of responsibility calls for teachers and administrators who are willing to take risks and who *expect* to make mistakes. The essence of creativity is daring to hazard mistakes. Someone once defined a genius as a "guy who gets into trouble for the sheer joy of getting out again." If students are to learn responsibility, they must be encouraged to get into predicaments and be helped to find solutions for them. This is the heart of the problem-solving method. There is little thrill in tackling problems where solutions are known in advance. True learning comes from tackling real problems within one's capacities and finding concrete solutions that can either be lived with or confronted as further problems for exploration.

DEALING WITH THE
CONSEQUENCES

Growth and learning to take on responsibility are often destroyed in youth through failures to permit "paying the piper." Part of the dynamics of learning responsibility is accepting the consequences of our own behavior. Feedback is an important part of learning in any area—academic, social, or personal. An important part of learning responsibility is experiencing what happens as a consequence of behaving a certain way or failing to behave at all.

Sometimes this important process is frustrated by well-meaning adults. They may interfere because they don't believe a child can handle the situation, because they hate to see a child face unpleasantness, or, perhaps, because they, themselves, have a need to be protective or controlling. For example, a teenager who found that his allowance would not make it possible for him to use his car as much as he would like discovered he could make extra money by collecting and selling scrap. One day, instead of offering to haul away excess junk from people's property as he usually did, he entered an abandoned property to pick up what he could. As he was carrying it off, he was arrested by the local police. In court the judge lectured the boy about getting his values twisted: "I think that running that car is much too important to you. I am therefore going to fine you $50.00 or you can turn in your driver's license for a month." The boy did not have $50.00 and was about to accept giving up his license when his father stepped in and paid the $50.00 fine. The teenager was thus prevented from learning a valuable lesson proposed by a wise judge. When his father was asked why he had paid the fine, he replied, "You know you can't keep kids from driving. I'd rather pay the fine than have him driving without a license."

Taking the consequences of our behavior is an important part of learning to be responsible. This does not mean, of course, that adults should sit idly by and watch a child suffer consequences so devastating that they might destroy or seriously injure him or her. Taking consequences is another form of problem solving and solving problems within one's level of capacity is the road to learning.

RESPONSIBILITY AND APATHY

Closely allied to the myth of irresponsible youth is the mythical complaint that students "are so apathetic." Apathy, it must be understood, is not a cause; it is a result. It occurs because personal meaning is absent. Blaming students for apathy is placing responsibility on the wrong persons. Responsibility for that condition must rest on the shoulders of curriculum makers and those responsible for introducing it to youth. Students, and people in general, are not apathetic when events they confront have value and meaning for them.[1]

Few of us will accept responsibility for events we have had no part in planning. It should not surprise us, then, that imposed events are likely to be resisted by truly healthy kids. Too much of teaching is little more than leading or herding kids down traditional pathways to foregone conclusions leaving little room for student exploration and discovery. A teacher friend of mine once said, "Good teachers never ask students questions the teachers know the answer to." Probably few of us can meet that criterion. That comment has provided me with much food for thought about my own behavior in the classroom.

Sometimes refusal to take responsibility is due to more than just a lack of interest. Parents and teachers might complain, "I wanted him to take responsibility but he wouldn't do it." The implications of such a remark are feelings of disdain for a youngster's lack of courage, or frustration that youth will not make the effort to achieve the values adults hold dear. But the problem may really be that the child has had so little prior success experience that the responsibility demanded of him, from his point of view, is simply too much. Most of us avoid getting involved in situations where failure seems certain. The solution to such predicaments is not to remove responsibility, but to build the child's capacity to deal with it through numerous success experiences at simpler, less frightening levels until a point of sufficient confidence has been reached to handle harder levels. Unwillingness to accept responsibility may not be intransigence or incapacity but lack of sufficient experience.

DYNAMICS OF LEARNING
RESPONSIBILITY

Teaching students to accept responsibility is a serious objective for education. It cannot be left to chance. The dynamics of learning responsibility are:

1. Responsibility is learned by personally solving problems. Progress should be from simple problems to ever more difficult ones as capacity increases.

2. Responsibility is a function of "owning" problems and dealing with the consequences.
3. Problems must be relevant and outcomes worthwhile.
4. Responsibility is fostered by an attitude that "it's good to look and fun to try."
5. A feeling of oneness and belonging with one's fellow human beings leads to feelings of responsibility for oneself and others.

Irresponsibility, like apathy, is not a cause of behavior but a result of lack of personal meaning and relevance. Schools can contribute to the dynamics of learning responsibility. Some do. Many more must contribute if education is to fulfill its mandate in a society dependent on responsible persons.

NOTE

1. E. C. Kelley, *In Defense of Youth* (Englewood Cliffs, N.J.: Prentice-Hall, Inc., 1962).

SELECTED READINGS

Brophy, J. E., and Good, T. L. *Teacher-Student Relationships: Causes and Consequences.* New York: Holt, Rinehart and Winston, 1974.

Combs, A. W. "Fostering Self-direction." *Educational Leadership* 23 (1966): 373–87.

Holt, J. C. *How Children Learn.* New York: Pitman Publishing Corporation, 1967.

Kelley, E. C. *In Defense of Youth.* Englewood Cliffs, N.J.: Prentice-Hall, Inc., 1962.

Moustakas, C. E., and Perry, C. *Learning to be Free.* Englewood Cliffs, N.J.: Prentice-Hall, Inc., 1973.

Neill, A. S. *Summerhill.* New York: Hart Publishing Co., Inc., 1960.

Nyberg, D. *Tough and Tender Learning.* Palo Alto, Calif.: National Press, 1971.

The Myth of the Power of Parents

A commonly heard cry in educational circles is, "What can you do with a child from a home like that?" This is the excuse teachers often use to express their frustration at being unable to achieve the goals they would like. It is never heard when those goals are reached. Teachers take credit for the splendid outcomes of schooling. They blame the parents when outcomes prove less than desirable. The myth of the power of parents is a handy excuse for failure.

PARENTS—LOW MEN
ON THE TOTEM POLE

Parental influence has not always been considered overpowering. Only a few hundred years ago, parents of an unruly child were looked upon as objects of sympathy because they had such a cross to bear. Having a problem child was often regarded as a visitation of the wrath of God for known or unknown sins.

It is only in more recent times that we have come to hold parents responsible for what their children become. Much of this new belief came about as a consequence of early studies in psychology. Freud and his colleagues, for example, pointed out the crucial importance of early experiences in the life of the individual. This understanding of the effects of early environment on a child's growth and development marked a long step forward in our understanding of how personality comes into being. It also established the myth of parent invincibility and started the greatest game of "pass the buck" in history. Colleges exclaim, "What can you do when students are graduated from high schools like this?" High schools, in their turn, bewail the fact that "Elementary schools are failing to prepare youth for high school!" And grade schools exclaim, "What can you do with a child from a home like that?" But parents, being low men on the totem pole, have no one to pass the blame onto. Parents are stuck with it. The best a mother can do is suggest that her child "really got it from his father's side of the family." Parents bear complete responsibility for whatever their children become. This myth is not only applied by educators. Judges, social workers, legislators, and even psychologists who ought to know better constantly exploit it as an excuse for all kinds of human failure.

THE EXPANDING WORLD
OF INFLUENCE

Like most myths, this one has a germ of truth. Parents *are* important to children. They do have early and vital influence on a child's unfolding personality. Each of us carries the effects of that early influence throughout our lives. But behavior and personality are not solely products of the past. A human being is never finished. Personality is the product of experience, *all* experience, including present experience.

As a child grows older, the world from which his or her experience is drawn grows larger and larger. The world of a newborn infant is a small one. It consists, almost exclusively, of mother and father. With growth and increasing awareness, however, the infant's world of significant experience begins to expand. Year by year it grows to include the child's siblings, relatives, people in the neighborhood, and eventually his or her school, city, nation, and the world itself. As the child grows older, parents become less and less significant as prime suppliers of experience. By the time he or she starts school, the modern child is already responding to a world far greater than that provided by parents. Parents are vaguely aware of this diminishing power. That is why mothers turn weeping from the schoolhouse door as they deliver their child to kindergarten for the first time. They know they will never again be as important in the life of their child as they have been. They have turned their child over to the world.

Human character and personality are built through experience, especially through interaction with the significant others in a person's life. This does not mean just one or two unforgettable experiences, but all experiences, including those a child has in school. Schools *can* be significant; that is why they were established. They can also be destructive or make no contribution at all, depending upon the beliefs of those who run them and the choices they make for action. With tongue in cheek Earl Kelley once said, "We have these marvelous buildings, this splendid equipment, magnificent curriculum, expert teachers and administrators, then, damn it all, the parents send us the wrong kids!" It is time we gave up that cop out and accepted children as they are delivered to us. Failure to accept that responsibility and realize the significant impact school has on all students can result in feelings of futility for school personnel, depressed morale, inadequate programs and, shabby expectations for students. All because of an inaccurate belief in the myth of the power of parents.

EFFECTS OF THE POWER
OF PARENTS MYTH

Neglecting "Problem Children"

The effects of the power of parents myth are especially insidious for children most in need of education's help and understanding. "Problem children," those to whom the what-can-you-do-with-a-child-from-a-home-like-that comment is most frequently applied, are usually problems because communication with parents has broken down. Demanding that the parents take full responsibility for helping such children may, in fact, be demanding help from the persons least able to provide it. When the relationship between parents and child has seriously broken down, it cannot be easily repaired, even by parents with the best of intentions. Human needs, wants, desires, and feelings do not change easily or quickly. Parents can legitimately be asked to *control* young children—to make them go to school, stay off the streets, observe the curfew, go along to visit Aunt Nellie—but to demand that parents behave therapeutically and provide the positive treatment experiences needed for a difficult child's recovery may be asking the impossible of an already bewildered and desperate father or mother. Educators who fail to understand these facts can generate abandonment of children by the very institutions established to care for them. Schools must do what they can with the children placed in their care. No child rejected at home ought to also be rejected at school.

Breaking Down Communication
Between Home and School

The myth of the power of parents has another unhappy effect. It contributes directly to the breakdown of communication between home and school by making school people angry at parents. Teachers, counselors, and administrators are rightly concerned about the child in school. This responsibility causes them to focus exclusively on the welfare of the child. As a consequence, teachers observing a child's disturbed reaction to some unhappy event, such as a divorce, may frequently be heard to exclaim, "Look at that! Can't they see what they are doing to that child?"—as though the parents *enjoyed* getting a divorce. Belief in the exclusive power of parents obscures the fact that a child's behavior is a product of his or her *total* experiences, both in and out of the family setting. It also ignores the dynamic character of families. Each person in a family affects everyone else. The personal problems of family members cannot be easily set aside in the interest of other members, even if one would like to do so. Parents, too, have problems, often problems that are traumatic and heartbreaking beyond belief. Children may be caught in the middle of such stress, innocent victims of the unhappiness swirling about them. This is not because parents want it that way. Such parents, themselves, are frustrated, suffering, and unhappy over the problems they confront. Least of what they need at such a time is someone getting angry with them, condemning them for their problems, and adding more guilt to already unbearable situations.

Parents, even bad ones, are necessary to children. Very few are so sick that they wish to destroy their children. The father who beats his child in a manner shocking to teachers may be doing it "because I want Eddie to be a good boy." Nothing's wrong with the motive; it's also what the teacher wants. Unfortunately, the all-powerful-parent myth makes teachers so angry, and concentrates attention so exclusively on the child, that understanding parents becomes hopeless and communication impossible. It also contributes to the myth that what teachers do is not important, discussed in Part III.

Belief in the power of parents can also interfere with home-school communication in another way. It makes teachers fearful of parents, especially parents of difficult students. As a consequence, parent interviews are likely to be avoided or entered into with fear and reluctance. Much of this fear is unnecessary. Parents of children in trouble are far more scared of teachers than teachers need be of parents. It is not an easy thing to have a difficult child. The myth has deluded parents, too. They believe they are totally responsible; they feel like failures, feel guilty and frustrated, and have a devastating concern for "what people will think." Small wonder they become defensive in interviews with school personnel. Sensitive understanding of such feelings by educators will go a long way toward relieving the teacher's own fears and contribute at the same time to the probable success of home-school communication. Whether we like it or not, schools must accept the responsibility for operating therapeutically with students committed to their care. Inaccurate beliefs about the power of parents should not interfere with that essential process.

SELECTED READINGS

Becker, W. C. *Parents are Teachers*. Champaign, Ill.: Research Press, 1971.

Bettelheim, B. "Where Self Begins." *Child and Family* 7 (1968): 5–12.

Bronfenbrenner, V. "The Roots of Alienation." *American Families: Trends and Pressures*. Washington, D.C.: U.S. Government Printing Office, 1973.

Ginott, H. *Between Parent and Child*. New York: Macmillan, Inc., 1968.

Gordon, T. *Parent Effectiveness Training*. New York: Peter H. Wyden, Inc., 1970.

PART III

MYTHS ABOUT
SCHOOL PRACTICES

All the myths explored so far in this book, those derived from American culture and those about the nature of persons, have inevitable effects on school practices. That's the way with basic assumptions: they exert their influence on all decisions that follow. But myths can exist on all levels of thinking, from the first dim glimmerings of concept development to the precise details of their expression in moment to moment practice. Education is no exception. Myths about actual school practices have developed and become accepted.

Critics of education have pointed out for generations that many traditional educational practices seem to exist for no clear or supportable reasons. They are easy to find in almost any school, but no one is quite sure where they started and because they have been around so long they have become sacrosanct. Innovations in education must withstand the closest scrutiny and the most skeptical judgments. Established practices, on the other hand, may go on for years with no one raising so much as an eyebrow about them. School practices must be continuously evaluated in the light of the best we know about the nature of students, learning, and the goals of education. If we do not make the effort to do this, we may unwittingly destroy what we have so carefully tried to contrive. One way to do this is to ask ourselves, our students, and everyone else responsible for policy and practice to examine whether school practices do, indeed, advance our primary purposes.

Every practice implemented in schools has inevitable side effects on educational goals, on teachers, and on students. Evaluation of practices must examine such side effects as well as immediate purposes. A teaching method that results in a measurable gain in grasp of subject matter at the expense of lowering student self-concepts, turning students off, or teaching destructive attitudes toward other people is clearly no bargain.

In the following part, a number of common myths about school practices are examined with an eye to their overall *effects on students and learning. The list is a short one; any teacher, parent, or administrator could no doubt add many more. The object in looking at these myths is not to put schools down. Like other myths, they need to be examined and understood so that truth may be separated from fiction and future practices designed on more promising bases.*

The Myth of the Affective Domain

One currently hears much talk in educational circles about "the affective domain." Most often this discussion originates with well-meaning persons who would like to see our public schools become more humane places. They point out that education needs to be more personalized, and to deal more effectively with affective aspects of learning such as student emotions, feelings, and values. There is no question that these goals are both desirable and necessary.

FEAR OF AFFECTIVE EDUCATION

Unfortunately, talk of the "affective domain" has become a red flag to many people who regard affective education as some sort of frill, a luxury most schools could just as well do without. Many parents, legislators, and members of the general public regard such talk as anti-intellectual. They see affective education as a dangerous departure from education's time-honored responsibilities to teach subject matter and skills and as a weakening of the vigor and discipline required for achieving those goals. Some people, believing that an educational system concerned with values is an unwarranted invasion of the traditional rights of home and religion, become nearly hysterical that the sacred prerogatives of church and family may be eroded. Others object to affective, humanistic education because it interferes with the goal of intellectual excellence. They deplore "education for adjustment" and demand we choose between education for intellect and education for adjustment, as though we needed to make a choice between smart psychotics and well-adjusted morons! If these objections were not enough the idea that schools should be concerned with emotion, feelings, and values is opposed by two well-entrenched myths already discussed in this book— the objectivity myth and the myth that if it's hard, it's good for you. In light of such educational, religious, and mythological traditions, it is not surprising that an educational system that talks about dealing with values is thought to be establishing dangerous precedents and neglecting its established functions to deal with matters that are none of its business.

THE NATURE OF EMOTION

Psychologists have news for those who decry affective education. They tell us that *all* behavior has affective qualities. Education must, therefore, be affective or there may be no education at all. Let's see why this is so.

Every human behavior carries some sort of feeling or emotion. The strength of that feeling is dependent on the personal meaning the matter being acted upon has for the behaver. The more important the matter, the stronger the feeling experienced. To observe this in action, imagine for a moment that you are a young woman with a lover off to war. He writes you that he is coming home in six months. Time passes and he writes that he will be home next month. Then, tomorrow he will be starting for home. Then, he is on his way. Now, he's back in the country. It's time to go to the airport!

Here comes his plane! There he is! One would be hardhearted, indeed, who did not feel an increasing emotional response in this series of events.

Psychologically, emotion is not a cause of behavior. It is a state of readiness that accompanies any human experience, a kind of acceleration that makes appropriate action possible. When we are asleep, for example, little energy is required. Like an idling auto engine, our motors are just turning over. When we awake and go about the tasks of the day, more energy is needed and our bodies respond by heightened tones and accelerated functioning. Confronted with events that seem personally threatening or enhancing, acceleration may rise to very high levels which are experienced as *excitement*, *fear*, *anger*, or *ecstasy*. Emotion is thus an indicator of the importance of events to us. I do not get very emotional about your child; I react very strongly about my own. In the earlier example of the young woman and her lover, the closer the anticipated event came to realization, the greater the degree of emotion experienced.

ALL LEARNING IS AFFECTIVE

Learning is the discovery of personal meaning. The basic principle of learning, as stated in perceptual psychology, is as follows: Any information will affect a person's behavior only in the degree to which he or she discovers the personal meaning of that information for him or her.[1] This discovery of meaning is always accompanied by degrees of feeling that increase as the relevance of events to self increases. There can be no such thing as an "affective domain" that is separate and apart from cognitive experience; cognition and emotion are inseparable. As we have already seen the presence of emotion is an indicator of the degree to which *any* learning has relevance to the self. If there is no personal meaning there is no feeling. If teaching does not change personal meaning nothing significant has really happened. The argument about whether education should be affective is a waste of time. The fact is, unless education is affective there will be no learning at all!

How students feel about subject matter, teachers, fellow students, school, and the world in general cannot be ignored. Emotion is part of the process of learning and is an indication of the degree to which real learning is occurring. Human attitudes, feelings, beliefs, understandings, and values can only be removed from the classroom at the risk of making what goes on in schools more irrelevant and less effective than ever.

Arguments about inclusion of the affective domain in the educational process are fruitless. Unfortunately, the term *affective* is, itself, enough to excite parents and teachers who see their goals and beliefs forwarded or repulsed by the concept. The whole idea has now been surrounded by such emotional connotations that we would all be better off if we dropped the term entirely. Few parents would argue with teachers' desires to make education more relevant. Most would also agree that helping children feel better about themselves and get along better with others are desirable objectives for education. Discussions couched in such explanatory language, avoiding the term *affective* altogether, can avoid a lot of headaches and contribute much more to effective communication.

The American public has established a long list of objectives for its public schools that cannot be achieved except through the exploration of values and feelings. Some of these are worthy home membership, concern for other people, reduction of prejudice, concern for democratic values, responsibility for self, getting along with others, and improving mental and physical health. To reach such worthy objectives, schools must deal with affective matters or fail in their responsibilities. The task is too big and too important to permit ourselves to be sidetracked by the myth of the affective domain.

NOTE

1. A. W. Combs, A. E. Richards and F. Richards, *Perceptual Psychology: A Humanistic Approach to the Study of Persons* (New York: Harper & Row, Publishers, 1976).

SELECTED READINGS

De Charms, R. *Personal Causation: The Internal Affective Determinants of Behavior.* New York: Academic Press, Inc., 1968.

Hamachek, D. E., ed. *The Self in Growth, Teaching, and Learning: Selected Readings.* Englewood Cliffs, N.J.: Prentice-Hall, Inc., 1965.

Kohlberg, L. "Stage and Sequence: The Cognitive-Developmental Approach to Socialization." *Handbook of Socialization Theory and Research.* By D. A. Goslin. Skokie, Ill.: Rand McNally & Company, 1969.

Lafferty, J. C. "Values that Defeat Learning." *National Association of Secondary School Principals Bulletin* 52 (1968): 201–12.

Lyon, H. C. *Learning to Feel, Feeling to Learn.* Columbus, Ohio: Charles E. Merrill Publishing Company, 1971.

Raths, L. E. et al. *Values and Teaching: Working with Values in the Classroom.* Columbus, Ohio: Charles E. Merrill Publishing Company, 1966.

Rokeach, M. *The Nature of Human Values.* New York: The Free Press, 1973.

Simon, S. B., Howe, L., and Kirschenbaum, H. *Values Clarification: A Handbook of Practical Strategies for Teachers and Students.* New York: Hart Publishing Co., Inc., 1972.

Weinstein, G., and Fantini, M. D. *Toward Humanistic Education: A Curriculum of Affect.* New York: Praeger Publishers, Inc., 1970.

The Myth that Competition
Is a Great Motivator

The myth of our competitive society (*see* page 15) finds expression in our schools in the myth that competition is a great motivator. Placing students in competition with each other in all kinds of settings is assumed to be an excellent means of inducing them to behave as expected, work harder, conform, and achieve ever higher standards of excellence. Students are required to compete for grades, seats in the classroom, places on the team, teacher's favors, "school privileges," and even places in line to go to the lunchroom, playground, or toilets. The belief in the value of competition as a motivator is rarely questioned and children are introduced to it almost from the first moment they step into school. From the kindergarten teacher's "Let's see who can be the quietest" at the beginning of a student's experience, to the university's award of degrees *cum laude, magna cum laude,* and *summa cum laude,* the student is manipulated, forced, seduced, and exhorted into competition in the firm belief that it is a prime motivation for learning.

COMPETITION AS A MOTIVATOR

As usual, the myth that competition is a great motivator contains an element of truth. Competition does, indeed, mo-

165

tivate *some* people *sometimes*. It also discourages and disillusions innumerable others. Psychologists know three things about competition as motive: (1) Competition is valuable as a motivator only for those people who believe that they can win; (2) People who do not feel that they have a chance of winning are not motivated by competition, they are discouraged and disillusioned; and (3) When competition becomes too important, morality breaks down and any means becomes acceptable to achieve desired ends.

Motivating People Who Believe They Can Win

People who enjoy competition and are exhilarated by it are those who feel they have a chance of success. No amount of effort can inveigle people who do not feel they can win into competing by choice. They avoid competition whenever they are able. Every teacher knows that the children who work for scholastic honors are the few who feel they have a possibility of winning. The rest sit back, let the competitors work like crazy, and, if they can, go about more important business of their own. Adults who feel they cannot achieve, as well as children, are quite content to let others make the effort. On any Saturday afternoon in the fall, one can find thousands of adults who need exercise gathered in football stadiums across the country to watch twenty-two players who don't need exercise get it. The motivational value of competition has been vastly overrated. Far from being a universal motivator, competition only serves to prompt those who are sure they can succeed or those who can be seduced into believing they have a chance.

Motivating People Who Do Not Feel They Have a Chance of Winning

Left to themselves, people will compete only rarely, and then only when they feel they have a chance of success. Forcing people to compete in spite of themselves can only result in discouragement, disillusionment, or rebellion. Forced to compete against her will, a child may simply go through the motions of doing a task in a dispirited, listless manner or break out in some form of opposition to her oppressors. When the cards are stacked against an individual, he will give up playing or start a fight with the people responsible for the stacking. It is only those who have been fairly successful competing in the past who value competition highly. People who do not feel able to win simply avoid competition to escape further humiliation.

A democratic society cannot afford a discouraged and disillusioned populace. People who feel inadequate to deal with life are, at best, a drag upon society and, at worst, an outright danger. An interdependent way of life like ours requires that people feel adequate and able. Techniques that discourage and disillusion students destroy human potential and prevent educational institutions from achieving the very goals for which they were established.

When Competition Becomes Too Important

The aim of competition is to win and the temptation is to win at any cost. Although it begins with the laudable aim of encouraging production, competition quickly breaks down to a struggle to win at any price. It is a powerful motivating force for those who think they have a chance of winning. But winning is a heady business that can become an end in itself, trapping the competitor in a net of his or her own making. When this happens people begin to cheat. In varsity sports, this appears in cutting corners, "playing dirty," and innumerable other devices for winning the game. The same thing happens in the classroom when grades become so important that students believe the only way they can make it is by cribbing on exams, plagiarizing papers, or pulling the wool over teachers' eyes.

Competition encourages lone wolf endeavors and lone wolves can be dangerous to a cooperative society. We need to be able to count on other people seeking our best interests along with their own. In the headlong rush to win, competition too easily loses sight of this responsibility. It produces aggression, hostility, and scorn. Dog eat dog becomes its philosophy. Too often the degree of glory involved for the victor is in direct proportion to the abasement and degradation of the loser. If education is truly to prepare people to live in our democratic society, it must be keenly aware of the negative aspects of competition and be on guard against them.

READING THE PRICE TAGS

The means we use to achieve our ends are always bought at a price. In competing, the price of winning may be more than we want to pay. We must read competition's price tags not only in dollars and cents, but in terms of human values, broken bodies, broken spirits, and disheartened and disillusioned people. In education, deciding what techniques to employ must always take into account the side effects of our actions. When the pharmaceutical industry develops a new drug, they carefully test its side effects before placing it on the market. After all, a drug that does a better job of curing a headache but makes one blind is not very useful. No matter how good their intentions or how promising a technique they may wish to employ, educators, too, must concern themselves with the side effects of their actions on students and teachers. This is especially true in respect to the motivational effects of competition. The myth of competition is so widely accepted in our society that one runs the risk of being considered un-American to question it.

A glance at contemporary education will make it apparent that competition is used at every level in our schools as a means of motivating students. More often than not, it is used in blanket fashion, applied to everyone with little or no regard for the diverse factors mentioned above. For the lucky few such treatment challenges, results are often excellent. For the great majority who are discouraged and disillusioned by competition, the outcomes are depressing to the students, deplored by their teachers, and generally written off as an indication of the student's lack of capacity, indolence, or perversity.

It is time we broke free of the myth that competition is a great motivator and learned to examine with greater care the full impact of the techniques we employ to motivate students. The motivating effects of competition are by no means universal so as to permit its use across the board. Its effects are dependent, not on what the teacher does, but on how the student feels about what was done. What seems challenging and exciting to the teacher may be a threatening, frightening prospect to the student. People feel challenged when confronted with problems that interest them and that they feel are reasonably within their capacities. People feel threatened when faced with problems they do not feel able to handle. (*See* the "Myth that If It's Hard, It's Good for You," on page 71.) The blind use of competition without clear understanding of its real effects on students may be expected of a naive apprentice. Truly professional people must understand the tools of their trade and use them with skill and precision. Bungling the use of tools is no more excusable in education than is the misuse of techniques in engineering, law, or medicine.

The basic need of all people is the maintenance and enhancement of the self.[1] This basic need is a built-in motivation for every human being. Students can be counted on to work very hard at matters that have relevance for them and that seem to be reasonably within their capacities for attainment. This fundamental need can be activated by teachers who understand youth and who use this understanding to confront young people with personally relevant problems paced to their readiness and capacities to handle them.[2] Such use of the student's personal need for achievement does not require comparisons with other **people**. The student's own need for fulfillment will keep him or her striving toward personal goals so long as he or she feels progress is being made and goals remain relevant and reasonably within reach. Motivational techniques built on these basic principles will motivate youth to excellence and at the same time avoid the invidious side effects of competition.

NOTES

1. A. W. Combs, A. C. Richards and F. Richards, *Perceptual Psychology: A Humanistic Approach to the Study of Persons* (New York: Harper & Row, Publishers, 1976).
2. A. W. Combs, ed., *Perceiving, Behaving, Becoming: A New Focus for Education,* 1962 Yearbook (Washington, D.C.: Association for Supervision and Curriculum Development, 1962).

SELECTED READINGS

Campbell, D. N. "On Being Number One: Competition in Education." *Phi Delta Kappan* 56 (1974): 143–46.

Grossack, M. M. "Some Effects of Cooperation and Competition upon Small Group Behavior." *Journal of Abnormal and Social Psychology* 49 (1954): 341–48.

Page, E. "Teacher Comments and Student Performance: A Seventy-four Classroom Experiment in School Motivation." *Journal of Educational Psychology* 49 (1958): 173–82.

Wax, J., and Grenis, M. "Conflicting Views on Competition." *Phi Delta Kappan* 57 (1975): 197–200.

The Myth of Grades and Grading

The use of grades to evaluate students is strongly entrenched in school tradition. The grading system has always been accepted without question as necessary, desirable, and helpful for students, teachers, parents, schools, and communities. Only in the last thirty years has anyone seriously begun to question the value of grades and grading more closely. The more people question, the more they recognize that the negative, destructive connotations of grading far outweigh whatever small positive values it possesses. Many schools at every level, from nursery school through university graduate schools, are finding ways to eliminate grades from the educational process.

People supporting the grading system generally argue that grading is necessary for two reasons: (1) its value in motivating learning, and (2) its value in evaluating student progress. A closer examination of these arguments finds them to be highly questionable.

GRADES AS MOTIVES
FOR LEARNING

As almost any teacher can attest, the value of grades as motives for learning is vastly overrated. Grades do not motivate most students very much—except for short periods, perhaps the day before they come out and one day after. The rest of the time, most students are little affected by the grading process. Human beings are highly unique and variable. If grades were truly significant motivators, then one would expect a student's grades to vary considerably from time to time. As a matter of fact, a student's grades remain almost constant throughout his or her school years. It is as though children learned their levels of expectation very early and thereafter filled their quotas.

Grades Are Based on Competition

Grades are essentially a form of competition. As we saw in our discussion of the "Myth of the Value of Competition," the motivating value of competition is restricted to those people who think they can win or who can be seduced into entering the contest. This principle applies to grades as well. The only students motivated to any extent by grades are those who feel they can earn high grades and who have come to value grades as indicators of prestige and status. The rest of the student body is not concerned about grades one way or the other.

Grades Are Artificial Reasons for Learning

People are naturally motivated to move toward health if the way is open to them. This was discussed earlier in the chapter on the "Myth that the Human Organism Can't Be Trusted." Applied to education, this means that students are always motivated to learn what they feel is significant and rewarding. One way to motivate students, then, is to make sure that the curriculum is relevant and the processes of learning are challenging. This is a direct, straightforward approach that requires adapting curriculum and methods of teaching to the peculiar needs of students.

Another way to motivate students is to set up *artificial*

reasons for learning in the form of grades and grading. Using this way, the curriculum and teachers can remain unchanged, while the students are seduced or coerced into learning by reward and punishment techniques that are unrelated to the significance or value of subject matter or ways of learning.

Of these two approaches to motivation, most schools have opted for the second, using grades as seductive lures for the willing students or as coercive weapons against the resistant ones. Artificial reasons for learning can never hope to compete successfully with real reasons. They are a temporary expedient at best. Once students become old enough to judge the relevance of what is being offered them, the value of grades as motivators may be lost entirely as students find innumerable ways to opt out, cop out, or drop out of the competition.

The myth of the value of grades has been with us a very long time. Grades have become a tradition and many persons, both in school and out, quite honestly believe a school cannot be run without them. A motivation technique that works for so few is surely most inefficient for a school system charged with the education of all children. Similarly, a method of motivation based upon artificial reasons for learning is hardly adequate for real students preparing to live in a very real world.

GRADES AS EVALUATORS
OF LEARNING

The Unreliability of Grades

The second major argument supporting the value of grades states that they are necessary to evaluate student progress. A careful examination of grades as evaluators, however, finds them little more valid in that capacity than as motivators. Grades are notoriously inaccurate. No two teachers grade on the same basis. Some teachers grade on how much progress the student has shown. Others grade on the amounts of subject matter mastered, tests taken, or projects completed. Still others compare a student's standing with his or her fellow students. Some even use grades for disciplinary purposes, marking a child on whether or not he or she has been "good." Hundreds of other factors having to do with teachers' purposes, goals, and values; student motivation; national norms; even such questions as which side of the tracks a child comes from, who his or her parents are, and how he or she is dressed or smells affect grades. Grades also vary widely from community to community, school to school, and in response to various forms of political pressure. Every teacher knows these things from personal experience. Yet, in spite of their notorious inaccuracy, grades are piously accepted as valid indicators of student status and progress. They are even accepted without question as the instruments for opening or closing the doors of schools and colleges.

An even more astonishing aspect of grades as evaluators is the bland assumption that a complex human being can be adequately described by a letter, number, or mathematical average. As one educator put it, "Isn't it a shame, with all the richness of the American language, we are reduced to evaluating a child *A, B, C, D!*" One would think that a truly adequate evaluative system would seek to describe its subjects in the fullest possible terms. If not that, then certainly, it should strive to describe them in the most important or characteristic aspects of their being and performing. Nevertheless, we continue to accept the narrow symbols of grades as significant and valid evaluations of persons and use them as bases for making far-reaching decisions about them.

Why Grades Are Supported as Evaluators

Grades are generally advocated as evaluators because they are useful for three different groups: the school administration, parents, and students.

The Convenience of Administrators. There is no doubt that grading provides a handy, convenient form of record keeping which lends itself readily to statistical treatment. In judging the value of grades, however, we must not consider only so narrow a base. Judgments about grading must take into account its effects on students and the learning process. If those effects are positive or neutral, the use of grades for administrative purposes is valid. If the effects of grades on students or the learning process are even mildly negative, that fact must supersede administrative convenience.

Reporting to Parents. Attempts to eliminate grades often run into great opposition from parents who honestly believe that grades are a necessary part of schooling. Having been through the educational system themselves, they want reports about their children in terms familiar to them. As a consequence, grades are often perpetuated simply to meet parental demands. Parents certainly need to know how their children are faring in school. What is more, in the interests of good communication, schools probably ought to provide parents the information they want in the form they want it. Schools have a further responsibility, however, that is to communicate to parents what cannot be conveyed in the sterile language of grades. Such matters might include the specifics of a student's successes or difficulties; special contributions the student has made to classroom activities; comments on the student's growth and development as a person; evidence of citizenship, concern for others, or leadership; the student's new interests and accomplishments; or anecdotal reports revealing aspects of the student's life in school in richer fashion than is possible by grades alone. Such matters should be reported as fully and completely as possible by whatever means of communication will best accomplish that purpose. If this is done well, parents, themselves, will soon discover the superiority of such communication over traditional grading systems.

Feedback to Students. As a device for helping students evaluate their learning, grades are completely inadequate by almost any criterion. Whatever small value using symbols to rate progress may have for a few students, it is completely overshadowed by their far greater negative effects on learning. Truly effective evaluation requires continuous information through which the student can determine where he or she is and where he or she needs to go next. Such information must also be specific and immediately related to student needs, purposes, and tasks confronted. Grades cannot hope to meet such criteria except upon the most tenuous and inadequate bases.

SOME SIDE EFFECTS OF GRADES

Grading practices can have very serious side effects on student attitudes and beliefs about themselves, other people, and the world in general. These far outweigh whatever small value grading possesses for teachers, parents, and administrators. Some of these side effects are the following:

1. Grades encourage students to work for the wrong goals.
2. Grades affect students' self-concepts.
3. Grades are a competitive device prone to the effects of competition.
4. The dedication of schools to grades and grading wastes the time and efforts of students, teachers, and administrators in order to feed the system.

Grades Encourage Working for the Wrong Goals

Psychologists know that the most effective learning is related to personal needs. Learning brought about by artificial reasons related to trumped-up needs is inferior to learning motivated by real, personal interest in the topics confronted.

Learning only to achieve high grades is usually temporary. Everyone who has been through school knows how to "psych" himself or herself for examinations. They also know how quickly such information is dissipated after the examination is completed. Knowledge without personal meaning has little relevance to life. We need only recall our own experiences in school, learning such things as the critical dates of the Civil War, how to diagram a sentence, how to solve a quadratic equation, or what the principal economic products of Wyoming are, to understand the impermanence of artificially motivated learning.

The Effects of Grades on Self-concept

An individual's self-concept plays a crucial role in human behavior. Because the self-concept is learned as a consequence of experiences in the process of growing up, what happens to children in school may have long-term effects on their beliefs about themselves. People learn that they are liked, wanted, acceptable, and able, or just the reverse, through the evaluations laid upon them in their formative years. The values placed on grades by parents, teachers, and the general public can become powerful indicators of personal worth from which students learn that they are bright, average, dull, incompetent, acceptable or unacceptable, good or bad, not just as students, but more broadly as persons.

Although they may be instituted with the best of intentions as means for evaluation, grades become little more than name calling, labels that tell the student who and what he or she is. Since people behave in terms of what they believe about themselves, such labels may also become self-fulfilling. We have already observed that student grades are like quotas that change very little once a child's level has been established during the early years of schooling. The world is full of people caught up in the circular effects of negative self-concepts. Believing they can only do X much, that is all they do. Others observing their behavior then exclaim "That is an X-much person." This only proves what the behaver believed in the first place. The human costs of inadequate or negative self-concepts are staggering throughout our society. Surely public schools ought not be involved in the production of such beliefs.

The Competitive Effects of Grades

Earlier in this book, we discussed the myth of the value of competition. Grades are essentially a competitive device that teachers hope will motivate learners to greater excellence. This outcome, however, is only achieved for the relative few who can be seduced into the competition. Students forced to compete in contests they feel they can't win are discouraged and disillusioned. Competition also encourages a dog-eat-dog conception of the proper way to live with one's fellows. This was dramatically emphasized for me some years ago when my son pointed out that, "Grading on the curve makes it to my advantage to destroy my friends." He also commented, "That's a hell of a thing to teach young people." We cannot afford a discouraged, disillusioned population or a citizenry so intent upon self-interest that it doesn't care what happens to others.

Grades Waste Time and Effort in order to Feed the System

Over the years, grading has evolved into a huge and involved system. Corporations have grown up to supply schools with tests, examinations, and devices that are in one way or another attached to the business of grading. Innumerable records must be kept and vast amounts of teacher time devoted to acquiring the data that feed the insatiable appetite of the grading system. Millions of man hours are used in discussions about grading practices, formulation of policy, dealing with inequities, etc., etc. All this effort might conceivably be worthwhile if there were clear-cut evidence of the value of grades in advancing learning or achieving greater excellence. The dedication of schools to grades and grading wastes much time and effort of students, teachers, and administrators solely to perpetuate itself. So vast an effort employed to support a system of such questionable value must surely represent one of the most important sources of inefficiency in education.

Kindergarten to graduate school, the use of grades for evaluating students is increasingly being replaced by other techniques. Ungraded primary schools and colleges are eliminating grades entirely or substituting pass-fail grading, no-fail record keeping, contract methods of problem solving, or any of a hundred other more appropriate forms of evaluation.

SELECTED READINGS

Educational Leadership. Entire issue devoted to alternatives to grading. 32 (1975): 243–304.

Kirschenbaum, H., Simon, S. B., and Napier, R. W. *Wad-Ja-Get? The Grading Game in American Education.* New York: Hart Publishing Co., Inc., 1971.

Krause, C. "Person-centered Evaluation Builds Positive Self-concepts." *Peabody Journal of Education* 49 (1972): 4, 290–94.

Lewis, J. *A Contemporary Approach to Non-graded Education.* West Nyack, N.Y.: Parker Publishing Company, 1969.

Mannello, G. "Grades Must Go!" *Education Record* 50 (1969): 305, 308.

McCarthy, R. J. *How to Organize and Operate an Ungraded Middle School.* Englewood Cliffs, N.J.: Prentice-Hall, Inc., 1967.

National Education Association Research Division. "Marking and Reporting Pupil Progress." *Today's Education* 59 (1970): 55–56.

Otto, H. J., Bowden, M. G., DeVault, M. V., Kotrlik, J. J., and Turman, J. A. *Four Methods of Reporting to Parents.* Austin, Texas: The University of Texas Press, 1957.

Pinchak, B. M., and Hunter, M. B. "Grading Practices in American High School. *Education Digest* 39 (1974): 21–23.

Silberman, A. "How Report Cards Can Harm Children and Mislead Parents." *Ladies Home Journal* 89 (1972): 72*ff*.

Simon, S. B., and Bellanca, J. A. *Degrading the Grading Myths: A Primer of Alternatives to Grades and Marks.* Washington, D.C.: Association for Supervision and Curriculum Development, 1976.

Strom, R. D. "School Evaluation and Mental Health." *Mental Health and Achievement.* Edited by E. P. Torrance and R. D. Strom. New York: John Wiley & Sons, Inc., 1965.

Wilhelms, F. T. *Evaluation as Feedback and Guide* (1967 Yearbook). Washington, D.C.: Association for Supervision and Curriculum Development, 1967.

The Fountainhead Myth

For most of human history, teachers have been persons who knew and helped others to learn what they knew. They were experts and their task was to impart their knowledge or skills to others. Even in the late nineteenth century, teachers were often the most knowledgeable persons in the community, at least with respect to academic matters. That role of the teacher, as the local fountainhead of knowledge, is now dead. Several contemporary events have done it in. Among these are: (1) the information explosion and the rapidity with which change occurs, (2) the fact that students know more now before they come to school, and (3) the fact that modern machines can provide information more effectively and efficiently than teachers.

THE INFORMATION EXPLOSION AND THE RAPIDITY OF CHANGE

The information explosion and the rapidity with which change occurs have killed for all time any hope that teachers will ever again be informed about more than a very small part of the information required to keep the world functioning. (*See* the "Myth that Knowledge Is Stable" on page 77.) Once, teachers considered it a disgrace not to know the answers to questions children posed. They honestly believed it was their responsibility to know. Many teachers still find it impossible to tell a student "I really don't know." They are still the victims of the belief that teachers should be fountainheads of knowledge. In a world of limitless information and ever-accelerating change, they are doomed to frustration and failure. The task they have set themselves is no longer humanly possible.

STUDENTS KNOW MORE
BEFORE THEY COME TO SCHOOL

Today's children are surrounded by sources of information not available to previous generations. Rising standards of living and ever-faster means of transportation have made it possible for people to go greater distances and see more. People do not live in the same place all their lives anymore. They scatter all over the country, even the world, and take their children with them. Even more important in providing information are television and movies. Television industry executives say that by the time the average American child is five years old, he or she will already have spent more hours watching television than he or she will spend in the first six years of school. Modern youths are bombarded with information everywhere they turn. They are likely to know a great deal more than their parents did at a similar age.

Teachers will often be confronted by students whose knowledge in many areas of human understanding vastly exceeds their own. This will be true even for the youngest children. A nursery school teacher recently complained that her students corrected her space terminology when she tried to tell them the story of man's first flight to the moon. "They were right," she said. "It brought me up short. They knew more about it than I did." With the explosion of information and the acceleration of change, such reversals of traditional teacher-student roles are bound to happen ever more frequently.

MACHINES CAN DO IT BETTER

Electronic gadgets have also made the teacher-as-fountainhead-of-knowledge concept obsolete. They can provide information far more effectively and efficiently than teachers. Students can be taken to a United Nations assembly by television. They can fight the battle of Bunker Hill side by side with the patriots through movies or watch the coronation of a monarch by satellite. Even facts and figures can be presented much better by any number of audio-visual devices. Libraries can now provide information on microfilm so that one can read original pages from newspapers long yellowed and faded or hear on audiotape a Roosevelt Fireside Chat. What teacher could hope to successfully compete with such devices in transmitting information?

If teaching is no more than providing students with information, then, indeed, teachers are obsolete. The assumption that teachers know and that children do not is no longer tenable as the basis for an educational system. Numbers of citizens believe that teaching requires no great skill, that it can be done by almost anyone. If teaching is defined simply as the providing of information, those people are probably right. There are other far more important reasons for teaching. The modern concept of teaching sees the teachers' role as one of facilitator of the learning process. It emphasizes teachers' functions as helpers, aids, assistants, guides, and friendly representatives of society. Teachers in this sense are not required to know all the answers. But, they must know how to facilitate and encourage the processes of learning. To do this well, teachers must be knowledgeable, of course. They also need an extensive understanding of students and their problems, accurate conceptions about the nature of the learning process, and appropriate beliefs about the purposes of schools and their own roles in teaching. With such understandings established, they further need creative ingenuity for putting all this together in ways to help each student grow to the maximum of his or her possibilities. As the public has long suspected, *anyone* can dole out information. It takes a real professional to meet the demands of modern conceptions of teaching.

If the teaching profession is to survive, it must give up the myth of the teacher as fountainhead of knowledge. The teaching profession must redefine its functions and purposes, not only to provide better reasons for existence in the eyes of the public, but, more importantly, to provide more adequate guidelines for the day to day operations in classroom, laboratory, or field.

SELECTED READINGS

Brown, G. I. *The Live Classroom.* New York: The Viking Press, 1975.

Collazo, A., Lewis, A., and Thomas, W. "Forecasting Future Trends in Education." *Educational Leadership* 34 (1977): 298–305.

Dexter, L. A. *The Tyranny of Schooling.* New York: Basic Books, Inc., Publishers, 1964.

Greer, M., and Rubinstein, B. *Will the Real Teacher Please Stand Up?* Pacific Palisades, Calif.: Goodyear Publishing Co., Inc., 1972.

Postman, N., and Weingartner, C. *How to Recognize a Good School.* Bloomington, Ind.: Phi Delta Kappa Educational Foundation, 1973.

Wees, W. R. *Nobody Can Teach Anyone Anything.* Garden City, N.J.: Doubleday & Company, Inc., 1971.

The Myth of Right Methods

Acting upon the assumption that there must be good or right methods of teaching, hundreds of researches have been designed to discover them. Millions of man-hours and hundreds of millions of dollars have been spent on such studies, but we are still unable to isolate any method or technique that is clearly associated with either good teaching or bad. One writer surveying the field was led to conclude:

> It is, I think, a sad commentary about our educational system that it keeps announcing publicly and privately that good and poor teachers cannot be distinguished one from the other. Probably no issue in education has been so voluminously researched as has teacher effectiveness and conditions which enhance or restrict this effectiveness. Nonetheless, we still read that we cannot tell the good guys from the bad guys.[1]

Another writer, commenting in the *Handbook of Research on Teaching*, says:

> Research ... has been abundant; hundreds of studies, yielding thousands of correlation coefficients, have been made. In the large these studies

have yielded disappointing results: correlations that are non-significant, inconsistent from one study to the next, and usually lacking in psychological and educational meaning.[2]

Despite this discouraging picture, research continues unabated. One group after another, burning with enthusiasm for some method that has worked for them, offers its peculiar technique, gadget, or organization as the new solution to the problems of educating young people.

THE ENDLESS SEARCH
FOR RIGHT METHODS

Over the years, we have seen education caught up in one fad after another. Among them have been teaching machines, phonics, teacher aides, audio-visual techniques, television, open classrooms, open schools, team teaching, and more recently, behavioral objectives, PPBS systems, and computer controlled instruction. Each has had a period of ascendance in which it was enthusiastically hailed as the universal panacea. It was soon discovered, however, that, while it had made some small contribution to a limited aspect of teaching, it was not going to save us after all. It was then filed away in the armory of teaching methods while we turned our attention with renewed hopes to the next star rising on the horizon.

Our inability to find a clear-cut set of right methods has been particularly disastrous for teachers' colleges. Without hard evidence of good and bad methods, teacher training institutions have had to rely on the experience, hunches, or philosophical bent of their particular faculties to determine what methods they will impart to their education students. Operating on the assumption that the methods of good teachers could be taught to beginners, they proclaimed the techniques of the particular experts they chose as models. Student teachers generally accepted this thinking and bravely sought to learn the models they were presented. Sometimes they were able to assimilate them into their own personality structure. More often, student teachers discovered that the methods they were taught did not work for them when applied in the classrooms they were assigned as professional teachers.

The search for right methods, it now becomes clear, is an exercise in futility. There are at least three very good reasons for this: (1) Methods must fit the teacher; (2) Methods must fit the conditions; and (3) Methods must be judged through the eyes of students.

Fitting the Teacher

Good teachers use highly divergent methods, yet all get good results. Therefore, it cannot be the methods that make the difference. Methods, we now understand, are highly individual matters. Like the clothes teachers wear, methods must fit the personality, philosophy, and purposes of the individual.

The methods teachers use arise from their own personal belief systems. Since teachers are highly unique, the techniques they use to express their beliefs and purposes must also be highly unique. The search for common methods is, therefore, doomed before it begins.

The crucial quality of methods is the *authenticity* or *fit* of the method for the teacher using it.[3] Methods are only vehicles through which the teacher's purposes are expressed. The methods of good teachers flow naturally and directly from the teachers' feelings, attitudes, beliefs, and purposes. Poor teachers' methods fail because they arise from faulty beliefs or because they are put on, acted by the teachers, and so convey a sense of uncertainty or phoniness to those they are intended to influence. Research at the University of Florida has demonstrated that teachers with clear and consistent belief systems can be effective with a wide variety of methods.[4] Teachers with confused or inadequate systems of belief will fail no matter what methods they employ.

Fitting the Conditions

Methods are tools for accomplishing teachers' purposes. It would seem self-evident that tools must be appropriate for the circumstances to which they are applied. Yet this principle is often violated as teachers attempt to apply a particular method without regard to the variability of the conditions under which they are applying it. No matter how fine a method is, it will fail if it is not appropriate for the conditions under which it is used.

A few of the factors determining choice of methods must certainly be:

1. **The Nature and Condition of the Student.** Students are notoriously variable. No two are alike. At the very least, they vary in ability, previous experience, physical condition, interests, attitudes, and readiness to confront whatever it is the teacher is trying to convey.

2. **The Nature and Conditions of the Work.** Methods must be adapted to the peculiarities of the environment in which the teacher operates. The same techniques are not appropriate for the playground, a field trip, or even the same classroom at different times of day. Equipment will also determine the kinds of methods to be employed. Heat, light, color, and space will affect the kinds of methods it may be fruitful to use.

3. **Policies and Procedures of a Particular School Organization.** While teachers have a good deal of latitude in choosing the methods they would like to employ, the policies, procedures, and expectations of supervisors, administrators, and the local community will also influence the methods chosen.

4. **The Nature of the Material To Be Confronted.** Methods must obviously be appropriate to the subject matter under consideration.

5. **What Has Gone Before and What Is Coming Up Next.** Methods must always be chosen in light of previous work accomplished and what is expected to happen next.

6. **Momentary Shifts in Conditions.** No one method can be expected to fit the multiplicity of conditions indicated above, especially when we add the necessity for making momentary shifts. An important distinction between the expert teacher and the novice is adaptability to changing conditions. Good teachers have the ability to drop a preconceived plan when necessary and shift to a better, more productive stance. They quickly judge the learning potential of unexpected occurrences and take advantage of the interest value of side issues or a humorous event. They quickly adapt to special opportunities to pursue a value question in the midst of an arithmetic lesson, to explore a concept not included in the syllabus of a history class, or to discuss the application of a general principle not thought of when the teacher composed his or her plan. Poor teachers are often the prisoners of their plans, doggedly pursuing their planbook outline to its bitter end.

Judging Through the Eyes of Students

Effective methods, in the final analysis, must not be judged in terms of what the teacher did or did not do or by how an outside observer viewed them. The effect of a given method must be judged according to what it meant to the student. If a student *believes* the teacher is unfair, it makes little difference whether the teacher really is or not. What matters is what the student experiences, not what someone else did or intended to do, and not how the application of a particular method is observed by some outsider.

THE EFFECTS OF TEACHERS'
BELIEFS ON STUDENTS

Research at the University of Florida indicates that good teachers can be clearly distinguished from poor ones on the basis of what they believe about people.[5] Good teachers, for example, generally believe that students are able; poor teachers have grave doubts about that. One teacher, believing her students are able, can require them to work very hard because she knows they can. Another good teacher may use a method that seems very lenient as he gives a child freedom to work on a problem as the child wishes because he has confidence in his student's basic ability. The message conveyed by each of these teachers is essentially the same—"My teacher thinks I can"—although the methods each employs are widely divergent.

The way teachers behave inescapably conveys their beliefs to the people they work with. I know a fourth grade teacher, a former officer in the Marines. He is a huge man who has a beautiful relationship with students who know, love, and respect him. I heard this man say to a child: "Hey, Jimmy. That's a pretty stupid thing to do!" Now, everything in my training and experience tells me that calling a child *stupid* is a destructive thing to do. But not for my friend! Jimmy answered his teacher by looking up at him in glee and saying: "Yeah. Wasn't it? Hee, hee!" Jimmy knew his teacher loved him and such a comment was only an indication that their relationship was so good they could josh each other without danger of getting hurt.

Methods must be understood as individual matters that teachers must explore and discover for themselves. This should be good news for teachers. They can be who they are, do their own thing, teach in their own best ways, and *still* be good teachers. It also means that teachers cannot be judged on the basis of the methods they use, nor can certain methods be demanded of teachers by supervisors, administrators, or the general public without running the grave risk of distorting or defeating the very goals they hope to achieve.

NOTES

1. D. E. Hamachek, "What Research Tells Us About the Characteristics of 'Good' and 'Bad' Teachers," in *Human Dynamics in Psychology and Education*, ed. by D. E. Hamachek (Boston: Allyn and Bacon, Inc., 1968), p. 187.
2. N. L. Gage, "Paradigms for Research on Teaching," in *Handbook of Research on Teaching*, ed. by N. L. Gage (Chicago: Rand McNally & Company, 1963), p. 118.
3. A. W. Combs, R. A. Blume, A. J. Newman and H. L. Wass, *The Professional Education of Teachers: A Humanistic Approach to Teacher Education* (Boston: Allyn and Bacon, Inc., 1974).
4. *See* the following:

   Robert G. Brown, "A Study of the Perceptual Organization of Elementary and Secondary Outstanding Young Educators" (unpublished doctoral dissertation, University of Florida, 1970);

   A. W. Combs, *Florida Studies in the Helping Professions*, Social Science Monograph No. 37 (Gainesville, Fl.: University of Florida Press, 1969);

   Charles Van Loan Dedrick, "The Relationship Between Perceptual Characteristics and Effective Teaching at the Junior College Level" (unpublished doctoral dissertation, University of Florida, 1972);

   Herman G. Vonk, "The Relationship of Teacher Effectiveness to Perception of Self and Teaching Purposes" (unpublished doctoral dissertation, University of Florida, 1970).
5. Ibid.

SELECTED READINGS

Aspy, D. N. *Toward a Technology for Humanizing Education.* Champaign, Ill.: Research Press, 1972.

Combs, A. W., Avila, D. L., and Purkey, W. W. *Helping Relationships: Basic Concepts for the Helping Professions.* 2d ed. Boston: Allyn and Bacon, Inc., 1978.

Ellena, W. J., Stevenson, M., and Webb, H. V. *Who's a Good Teacher?* Washington, D.C.: American Association of School Administrators, National Educational Association, 1961.

Frymeir, J. H. *The Nature of Ec cational Method.* Columbus, Ohio: Charles E. Merrill Publishing Company, 1965.

Gage, N. L. *Handbook of Research on Teaching.* Chicago: Rand McNally & Company, 1963.

Getzels, J. W., and Jackson, P. W. "The Teachers' Personality and Characteristics." *Handbook of Research on Teaching.* By N. L. Gage. Chicago: Rand McNally & Company, 1963.

Jackson, P. W. *Life in Classrooms.* New York: Holt, Rinehart and Winston, 1968.

The Myth that What Teachers Do Is Not Important

Closely allied to the power of parents myth is the myth that what teachers do is not important. In addition to the cry, "What can you do with a child from a home like that," teachers and administrators bewail the forces exerted on youth by television, the community, student peers, athletics, and a hundred other outside pressures. They complain that influences outside the school are so powerful, what goes on in school cannot possibly hope to make a difference. It is true that students are the products of many more forces than those they encounter in the classroom. The belief that schools can't hope to make an impact in light of such outside forces is completely false.

EXPERIENCE IS FOREVER

Human experience is not reversible. We cannot unexperience what we have already experienced. Every good experience each teacher gives a child is given that child forever. To be sure, many outside influences are also working on children, sometimes in opposite directions, so that experiences in school may not be enough to result in immediate changes in student behavior. But that does not mean that school experiences are unimportant or without effect.

Human beings are the products of all their experiences. Each person is a walking economy. As he or she moves about the world some things that happen make deposits in his or her account; others make withdrawals. Some lucky people have large numbers of positive experiences and so accumulate vast assets. Others, unhappily, have so many negative experiences, their accounts are drained and they are forced into the bankruptcy of negative self-concepts and feelings of inadequacy, of being unloved or unacceptable. Fortunately, most kids come out fairly even, but there are always some children in any school who are suffering serious deficits in positive experience. Maladjustment, we know, is a problem in deprivation. It comes about because a person is unable to achieve some measure of personal fulfillment. Serious deprivation over long periods of time does dreadful injury to the human personality and results in mental illness or the hostility and anger of delinquency and crime. (*See* the "Myth that They Like It That Way" on page 97.)

A deeply deprived child requires a lot of deposits to balance withdrawals being made in other parts of his or her experience. This fact can be a discouraging thing for well-meaning teachers who see their very best efforts apparently being negated by people or events elsewhere in a child's life. Observing no change, it is easy to conclude that one's own efforts are useless. But deposits are *never* in vain. Even when they are not enough to turn the balance, they strengthen and buttress a child's resources to meet the difficulties encountered elsewhere. Good experiences counter bad experiences. The opposite is also true. One can build a better account by making more and bigger deposits or by preventing withdrawals. Teachers may not be in position to prevent withdrawals, but there is no one to stop them from making deposits except themselves.

PEOPLE DO NOT
CHANGE QUICKLY

Teachers often defeat themselves by expecting too much too soon. This is especially true in dealing with difficult students. Take the case of a tough delinquent who, over a period of fourteen years, has thoroughly learned from hundreds of personal experiences: "Nobody likes me. Nobody wants me. Nobody cares." He has come to the conclusion, "I don't care about nobody neither!" Such a deprived and hostile youngster is not likely to respond immediately and positively to some nice comment a teacher makes to him on a Wednesday afternoon. What often happens goes something like this:

> With the best of intentions the teacher makes a complimentary comment. In light of his past experiences, the student sees the comment as a lie, a put down, a mockery, or (because he would like so much for it to be true) too much to handle. He responds to the teacher in ways appropriate to those feelings —defensively, with anger, hostility, defiance, or a "smart aleck" retort. The teacher, finding his overtures rebuffed, responds in turn with anger, rejection, or disciplinary action. This proves to the youngster what he already thought in the first place, "You don't like me either."

So the teacher and the student passed each other like ships in the night for lack of understanding of how things look from the other person's point of view. The teacher defeated himself right from the beginning by expecting too much too soon.

It takes time to change and the more important the characteristic to be changed, the longer it takes. Helping a child change his conceptions about the length of the Amazon River is no big deal. Producing a change in how he or she feels about himself or herself, or about school experience is quite another matter. School people who do not understand this basic principle are likely to create their own frustration and discouragement. Feelings of futility, in turn, guarantee that little positive action is likely to be taken. Worse still, such feelings may cause teachers and administrators to act in ways that make problems worse for students already in trouble.

TEACHERS CAN MAKE
A DIFFERENCE

Teachers can make very important contributions to a child's growth and development, even for the sickest, most difficult child. Even a mere holding operation may be the first step to better things. When everything else in a child's life is pushing him downhill and all a teacher can do is help him stay as bad as he is—that's progress! If a teacher's efforts do no more than counter negative forces the child is experiencing elsewhere, that teacher's efforts are not in vain.

Good experiences in school can even change the outside circumstances affecting a child. Success experience with arithmetic, geography, or any other subject can be therapeutic. Positive experiences in school can make the blandishments of drugs or the influence of peer group pressures seem less fulfilling and attractive.

Success in school can even produce changes in a child's homelife without the teacher ever going near it. I have more than once seen the dynamics of that process operate like this:

> A mother and father are driven frantic by a difficult child. The child comes to school and is difficult there, too. But somewhere in the school setting he develops a relationship with a teacher who helps him gain a small measure of respect for himself and a glow of success experience. As a consequence, the child goes home to his family in better humor. Be-

cause he feels better about himself, he doesn't bug his mother quite as much. This takes pressure off the mother. She is relieved to find that she and her son are getting along better. When the father comes home, she doesn't take her frustration out on him, as she usually does. The father, finding the "old lady" is easier to live with today, is more relaxed and deals with his son in a more pleasant, accepting fashion. The child does not know why his father is more pleasant and caring, but he feels better about his father and behaves better toward him, too.

A family is a dynamic unit in which each person affects each other person. Changes in each member are mirrored in all the others. Many a teacher has made changes in a family such as those described without ever knowing it.

Children learn and grow as a consequence of experience with significant others they encounter in life. Schools and teachers *can* be significant others in the lives of students. They can also be insignificant, even negative, others. The kind of influence school people exert on students will be dependent upon the choices they make and the assumptions from which they make those choices. Schools do not have to be futile unless school people make them so. A firm belief in the myth that what teachers do is not important is a sure way to guarantee that the myth will turn out to be true.

SELECTED READINGS

Aspy, D. N., and Roebuck, F. N. *Research Summary: Effects of Training in Interpersonal Skills.* Washington, D.C.: National Institutes of Health, 1974.

Gorman, A. H. *Teachers and Learners: The Interactive Process.* Boston: Allyn and Bacon, Inc., 1969.

Lewis, A. J., and Miel, A. *Supervision for Improved Instruction: New Challenges, New Responses.* Belmont, Calif.: Wadsworth Publishing Co. Inc., 1972.

Moustakas, C. *The Teacher and the Child.* New York: McGraw-Hill, 1956.

Rogers, C. R. *Freedom to Learn.* Columbus, Ohio: Charles E. Merrill Publishing Company, 1969.

Schaefer, R. J. *The School as a Center of Inquiry.* New York: Harper & Row, Publishers, 1967.

PSST!

The Myth that They Won't Let Me

Whenever the necessity for change in education is under discussion, "I would, but they won't let me" is heard. More often than not, the *they* referred to is some generalized other, some vague, undefined ogre who disapproves of the good things people would like to do and prevents them from making the changes they would really like to make. This myth, of course, is not limited to education. The complaint that "they won't let me" can be found in the way of progress everywhere. Wherever it appears, it is, more often than not, false.

A HANDY EXCUSE FOR INACTION

All of us, including teachers and school administrators, have far more freedom to innovate than we like to believe. The myth that they won't let me is really a handy excuse for inaction. It even has advantages. Instead of having to blame ourselves for inaction, we can see ourselves as really splendid persons who would do great things if only we were allowed to do so. Other people, believing the complaint is real, may even feel sorry for us or express their admiration for our steadfastness in the face of opposition.

The interfering *they* is not always imaginary. Sometimes

it may be true that some person or persons can actually be found who would forbid a proposed activity. More often than not, however, when the interfering *they* is traced to some specific person, the opposition ascribed is found to be nonexistent. As a consultant, I have often listened to teachers voice their reasons for not attempting some innovation. Later, while talking with their principals or administrators I would ask, "How come you will not let your teachers do thus or so?" Frequently I received the reply: "You're kidding! I've been hoping they would do something like that for the last five years."

The problem of changing American education is immense. An institution involving several million teachers and 40 or 50 million students is not about to change over night. Neither is it going to be changed significantly from the top by administrative regulation. Whatever changes occur must come from the teachers themselves. In the final analysis, it is they who control what goes on with students. Unless teachers change, there will be no change, as many a frustrated administrator or supervisor can attest from sad experience. Teachers need to understand their crucial position as agents of change. The myth that they won't let me must not be permitted to discourage innovation. The need to bring our schools more closely in touch with current society is much too great.

RESISTANCE TO CHANGE

Bureaucracies have an innate tendency to protect themselves and resist change. This is especially true in education with its fear of mistakes and its age-old emphasis on being right. Confronting the need for change produces anxiety. The normal reaction to anxiety is to avoid it whenever possible. Administrators and supervisors, therefore, may react to the suggestion of an innovation by not wanting "to make waves" or "to rock the boat." Anxiety is the source of much of the opposition *they* impose on their staffs. It is no wonder teachers who have experienced it soon begin to assume *they* will surely object to new ideas before the teachers have even suggested them. As a lifelong experimenter in education, I have learned to deal with such generalized opposition by never asking permission to make an innovation unless it is absolutely necessary. I have learned to make changes as quietly as possible, without fanfare, while at the same time taking care to accumulate evidence demonstrating the superiority of the new procedures over the established ones. The longer the innovation continues in this fashion, the less likely it is that anyone will ever raise a question about it. People unconsciously adapt to its presence and before long it is accepted as normal.

An innovation already in being is difficult to oppose, particularly if clear evidence of its superiority is also at hand. Authority figures inclined to force the innovator to return to where he or she was must face the necessity of making more changes to get back where things were. This is upsetting. The very resistance to change that would have prevented the innovation in the first place now works to keep it in existence. When authority figures have sometimes complained that what I was doing was out of line, I have been able to support the value of an innovation by evidence of its superiority over existing practice and by the enthusiastic support of those involved. In the face of such data, administrators will find it difficult to insist on returning to less effective practices. In my own experience, the authority figure and I usually resolve our discussion by working together to find a way to "make it legal."

Trying to solve administrative problems in advance by assuming that "they won't let me" blocks innovations before they even get off the ground. The proper task of administrators is to solve problems and facilitate processes. If they do not know that problems exist, they may go on forever in the delusion that everything is "just fine." Operating on that assumption, they report "No problems" to their superiors with the result that nothing can happen at that level either. Teachers need to *create* problems for administrators. Administrators have the right to reject proposals, but teachers can rob both themselves and the administrators of opportunities to consider innovations by assuming they won't let me before making certain that that is truly the case.

THE TEACHER'S "WRIGGLE ROOM"

Teachers have far more freedom to innovate than they ever use. When the classroom door is closed, nobody, but nobody, knows what is going on in there except the teacher and the students. And most of the time the students aren't sure! Teachers may not be able to change the educational system, their school, or their administrator, but the variations possible within an ordinary classroom are almost limitless. Many innovations can be started without other people's knowledge or approval simply by assuming that the action taken is necessary to carry out one's professional responsibilities.

My friend Lance Hunnicutt used to say: "In any situation there is always room to wriggle. If you would like to find out how free you are, try wriggling." The point is well taken. If one takes up the slack in his or her "wriggle room," others get used to him or her being there and unconsciously provide a little more slack. By consistently taking up the slack in the same direction, a great deal of progress can be made with no one aware that changes have been made. By the end of a year, such step-by-step progress may result in a surprising amount of change. Even if others become aware that a teacher has moved from there to here, nobody is quite sure how it happened.

The need for innovation in education is long overdue. The inertia of bureaucracy is hindrance enough. We cannot afford to discourage progress by creating additional blocks that do not exist. What is needed is honest assessment of what can be done and the wit and the will to get about doing it. If we don't make the effort to unshackle ourselves, we deserve our chains.

SELECTED READINGS

Gardner, J. W. *Self-Renewal: The Individual and the Innovative Society.* New York: Harper & Row, Publishers, 1964.

Jackson, P. *Life in Classrooms.* New York: Holt, Rinehart and Winston, 1968.

Moustakas, C. *The Authentic Teacher: Sensitivity and Awareness in the Classroom.* Cambridge, Mass.: Howard A. Doyle, 1966.

Rogers, C. R. "A Plan for Self-directed Change in an Educational System." *Educational Leadership* 24 (1967): 717–31.

The Myth of the Value of Grouping

Teachers have always sought ways to group students for greater convenience and for efficiency in teaching. With the decision to educate everyone and the establishment of public schools, the search for methods of grouping students became much more intense. It continues unabated to the present day. Every sort of arrangement to deal with numbers of students at once has been explored. Some have been mere fads, appearing on the scene for a short time only to be replaced by other more loudly proclaimed solutions. Others have been accompanied by emotional opinions on both sides. Some have even become public issues with whole communities involved in the debate. The argument over whether children should be grouped heterogeneously or homogeneously, for example, can still produce heated discussion in many communities.

RESEARCH ON GROUPING
IS DISAPPOINTING

Most grouping methods are advocated on the grounds that they improve learning and contribute to student growth and development. In reality, the ways students are grouped have little or nothing to do with efficiency in learning. Hundreds of studies on every conceivable method of grouping have been carried out over the past fifty years with completely disappointing results. For example, in a survey relating grouping to pupil learning in 1966, Franseth and Koury concluded:

> Over the years attempts have been made to group children according to ability as a way of fostering progress in school achievement. Many research studies have been conducted to test the belief that children will succeed better if the range in ability in a class could be reduced. However, results indicate that this method of dealing with children's learning has not been productive. Franseth and Koury found that available evidence indicates that factors other than the particular grouping methods used account for differences in achievement gains between children grouped according to ability and those grouped heterogeneously.[1]

In another study, after a comprehensive review of the research on ability grouping, Findley and Bryon made the following conclusions:

a. Homogeneous grouping by ability across the subjects of the school curriculum is impossible. Groups homogeneous in one field or sub-field will prove heterogeneous in other fields. Thus, children grouped by reading score or "intelligence" will overlap considerably in mathematics achievement.

b. Ability grouping, as practiced, produces conflicting evidence of usefulness in promoting improved scholastic achievement in superior groups, and almost uniformly unfavorable evidence for promoting scholastic achievement in average or low-achieving groups. Put another way, some studies offer positive evidence of effectiveness of ability grouping in promoting scholastic achievement in high-achieving groups; studies seldom show improved achievement in average or low-achieving groups.

c. The effect of ability grouping on the affective development of children is to reinforce (inflate?) favorable self-concepts of those assigned to high achievement groups, but also to reinforce unfavorable self-concepts in those assigned to low achievement groups.

d. The effect of grouping procedures is generally to put low achievers of all sorts together and deprive them of the stimulation of middle-class children as learning models and helpers.[2]

Reviewing the research available leads to the conclusion that there is no method of grouping that can be clearly shown to be superior to any other method of grouping or of nongrouping. There is good reason why these disappointing results occur. The way students are grouped for learning is only a method of teaching. We have seen elsewhere in this book that right methods are a myth. (*See* the "Myth of Right Methods" on page 191.) Learning is a complex internal process affected by a wide variety of factors both inside and outside the learner. The particular group setting in which learning occurs, like any other method applied to teaching, is but one small factor among many determining what goes on inside a student. People can learn or not learn in all kinds of groups or in no group at all.

GROUPING IS AN
ADMINISTRATIVE EXPEDIENT

How students are grouped for teaching is not a dynamic of learning, it is an administrative expedient designed to help teachers and administrators carry out their tasks. Administrative expedients are perfectly legitimate and must be judged in terms of their practical usefulness. Whether or not a mode of grouping contributes to effective learning is quite another matter; this must be judged in terms of the effects the method has on each individual student. Since students are infinitely unique, and grouping is a device for treating people "in common," it is clear from the start that no method of grouping can ever meet the individual needs of students. To search for a common uniqueness is impossible by definition.

CRITERIA FOR GROUPING

Once we have accepted the fact that (1) grouping is an administrative expedient without magical qualities in its own right, and (2) the value of grouping must be evaluated in terms of its effects on individual students, it becomes clear that the primary basis for grouping must be the readiness of the student for the particular task to be confronted. Beginning with that understanding, many kinds of grouping make sense, from the highly volatile, rapidly forming and breaking groups of nursery and kindergarten children to the stable groups of college students registered for a class in "American History—1780 to 1830." A wide variety of grouping patterns are possible, varying with such student conditions as age, interests, mood, goals, values, and feelings toward colleagues. They may also vary with teachers' purposes, feelings of security, preferred ways of teaching, relationships with students, and mastery of materials and with the peculiar environments, equipment, and supplies available.

Counter-indications for Grouping

Within the basic principle of grouping according to the readiness of the student, some practices are highly questionable. A few of these must certainly be: (1) grouping on the basis of intelligence test scores, (2) permanent grouping, (3) segregative grouping, and (4) grouping by age and grade level.

Grouping by Intelligence Test Scores. Intelligence tests are designed as *blanket* indicators of *general* student aptitude. As such, they cannot possibly meet the criterion of student readiness for a particular task to be confronted. They are crude instruments at best, inappropriate for the precise individual information needed for proper grouping. While sometimes useful for indicating the general level of performance to be expected from a class or school, they are notoriously inaccurate when applied to individuals. The use of such instruments may do incalculable harm to students grouped on such inadequate bases.

Permanent Grouping. Grouping students permanently within a school or institutionally in separate schools can only result in injustice and injury to many students. Readiness for learning is not a permanent thing. The readiness of students to confront tasks is a highly variable matter, subject to enormous changes because of factors such as time, interests, attitudes, experience, growth, and opportunities to learn. An educational system truly dedicated to helping students achieve the maximum of their potentialities cannot afford to permit grouping practices to be frozen. Practices must remain optimally open and fluid.

Segregative Grouping. A method of grouping that separates a student from his or her legitimate peers on any continuing basis is more damaging than helpful. As a nation we are committed to the principle of equality for all people no matter what race, creed, or color they are. Methods of grouping that isolate students from one another on such bases must be abhorred by our public school system. Methods of grouping that isolate students from their fellows, no matter how good the intentions behind that method, do more harm than good when seen in a broader perspective.

Side effects of grouping methods must always be an important consideration when evaluating the usefulness of a particular method. This is true even for students segregated on the basis of scholarship. As a psychotherapist working at the college level, I have often picked up the pieces of students classified as gifted in the elementary grades who were thereafter assigned to special programs for the rest of their years in school. I vividly recall their distress as they sobbed, "I find myself prepared for a world that doesn't exist." The experience of growing up interacting with many different types and levels of people is, itself, an important preparation for living successfully with one's fellows in the broader society beyond school.

Grouping by Age and Grade Level. A major criterion for grouping children throughout our public schools is age and grade level. If we accept the readiness of the student to confront tasks as the primary criterion for grouping, then, surely, these two determiners for grouping are the least applicable and least appropriate bases for organizing learning. The readiness range in children at any given age or grade level is so great we cannot hope to group students effectively on this basis. To do so can only result in depriving all but a few students of opportunities fitted to their personal needs and conditions. Despite this obvious fact, observable by any teacher, our schools continue to use age and grade as legitimate criteria for grouping students. The myth of the value of grouping dies hard.

NOTES

1. J. Franseth, and R. Koury, *Survey of Research on Grouping as Related to Pupil Learning* (Washington, D.C.: U.S. Government Printing Office, 1966).

2. W. G. Findley and M. M. Bryon, *Ability Grouping: 1970, Status, Impact and Alternatives.* Athens, Georgia: University of Georgia, Center for Educational Improvement, 1971), pp. 2, 3.

SELECTED READINGS

Haberman, M., and Raths, J. "High, Average, Low—And What Makes Teachers Think So. *Elementary School Journal* 68 (1968): 241–45.

Haderman, K. F. "Ability Grouping: Its Effects on Learners." *NASSP Bulletin* 60 (1976): 85–89.

Schrank, W. R. "The Labelling Effect of Ability Grouping." *The Journal of Educational Research* 62 (1968): 51–52.

Schrank, W. R. "Further Study of the Labelling Effects of Ability Grouping." *The Journal of Educational Research* 63 (1970): 358–60.

Weinstein, G., and Fantini, M. D., eds. *Toward Humanistic Education: A Curriculum of Affect.* New York: Praeger Publishers, Inc., 1970.

The Grade Level and Class Size Myths

When public education was very young, schools were organized around the needs of the neighborhood. All the children who needed educating were sent to the local school to be taught by a teacher hired for that purpose. No one worried much that students varied in age and ability. They all went to one- or two-room schools and were taught by teachers who were expected to help them learn whatever they were ready for. A single room might include children aged five to eighteen, working on subject matter ranging from kindergarten to high school. No one suggested it couldn't be done. They just went ahead and did it.

As our population increased, schools began to be organized in grade levels; classes were established around one teacher and about thirty students. This was done in order to make schools more efficient and to provide enriched experiences for students. In time this organization by grade level and conception of proper class size, which began as an administrative expedient, became frozen into tradition.

THE GRADE LEVEL MYTH

An Administrative Expedient

The assignment of students to standard class sizes and grade levels is simply a method of grouping, an administrative expedient without inherent intrinsic value for learning. It is a matter of convenience for teachers and administrators. It has little or nothing to do with the learning process except, perhaps, to make it more difficult for students.

The organization of children into age-grade levels runs directly contrary to everything we know about human variability. Age and grade level are two of the least significant factors for distinguishing children from one another. Even after children have been sorted into age or grade-level groups, hundreds of other factors remain uncontrolled to guarantee enormous diversity in any class.

Eliminating these uncontrolled factors is impossible. We have been trying to find ways of grouping children to eliminate human variability since the earliest days of public education. Today we are no closer to solving that riddle than we were one hundred years ago, but we still persist in the effort. It is time we gave it up and buckled down to the business of finding ways to personalize instruction. This suggestion is usually met by loud cries that it can't be done. That, of course is ridiculous. American education began in the one-room school where children of every level of competence and readiness worked under a single teacher. Our teacher grandmothers did it; we can too.

One Effect of Grade Level Organization: Social Promotion

Adherence to grade-level organization results in all sorts of confusion for teachers and the public. Most schools have long since given up promoting or not promoting children on the basis of performance. Children are moved along year by year no matter how their performance compares with their peers. This has led to great storms of argument over the question of "social promotion." The public believes that grade levels mean something and schools should stand by them, promoting students or holding them back on the basis of their grade level performance. Strict adherence to grade level organization, however, has an unhappy side effect. Skipping the bright students forward while holding the dull ones back inevitably results in dropping the average level of teaching throughout the system. This is because dull students are kept in school while bright students are pushed out.

Research on promotion and failure clearly indicates that holding children back to repeat a grade while their friends move ahead has very unwholesome effects on their behavior and adjustment. As far back as 1944, Sandin reported that nonpromoted children exhibited more troublesome behavior, and were more inattentive, less cooperative, more easily discouraged, and worried about their failure.[1] Nonpromotion puts a child into a situation where it is difficult to adjust. Often this leads to the child leaving school entirely. H. A. Caswell and A. W. Foshay cite a number of research findings that show that children with failing grades who are promoted actually exhibit greater progress than similar pupils who are held back.[2] Clearly, the enforcement of grade-level standards defeats its own purpose.

Organizing classes by grade level ignores human variability. It organizes learning around subject matter without regard to student readiness or capacity. Instead of adjusting the subject matter to the student, it insists the student adjust to content. The inadequacy of such a plan for effective learning should be apparent to anyone. A public system of education must take each child as he or she comes and help each young citizen achieve the maximum of his or her potential. Subjecting students to curricula that do not fit their needs and current situations is forcing the well-known round pegs into square holes. Such a system is doomed to mediocrity, forever defeated by its own false assumptions.

Some Side Effects of Organization by Grade Level

A proper evaluation of grade level organization must take into account the side effects it imposes on students and learning. Among the most blatant, the following must certainly be reckoned with:

1. It discourages and disillusions students who fall behind grade level expectations. The child in sixth grade, for example, who is reading at third grade level is subjected to daily doses of failure with inevitable effects on his or her self-concept and outlook on the world.
2. It fails to challenge brighter students. Growth is stimulated by reaching for problems just beyond one's current grasp. Endless repetition of what is already known results in apathy and boredom.
3. It separates peers on the basis of unnatural, irrelevant criteria. The real world of children is not standardized. Children's normal society includes a wide spectrum of persons and traits, just like the adult society they will one day join.
4. It restricts the range of curricula to that deemed "right" by history and tradition. Because human beings and human needs are so insatiably diverse, a personalized curriculum must necessarily be far richer, more diverse, and more effective in meeting the needs of students.
5. It inhibits the creativity of teachers and students alike by discouraging innovation and narrowing the range of exploration.
6. It violates the basic criterion of grouping—the need to take into account the variability of students and their readiness to confront the material about to be presented.
7. Most important, it encourages educators to avoid the necessity for personalizing instruction.

The myth of grade level organization causes more trouble than such an administrative expedient is worth.

THE CLASS SIZE MYTH

Many of the comments we have made with respect to grade level organization apply to the class size as well. For several generations we have lived with the idea that there is a proper size for classes in public education—generally a figure in the neighborhood of thirty students, plus or minus five per teacher depending upon the school examined. The concept of a most-efficient class-size has existed so long, it has acquired the stamp of tradition. The proper number of students per class varies locally within the mentioned range, but whatever the local figure is, it is stoutly defended as necessary for efficient learning and administration. The standard class size figure has been argued continually over the years. Teachers insist they cannot teach effectively unless it is lowered; administrators and school boards maintain just as stoutly that it ought to be increased in the interest of balanced budgets and efficiency. The idea that there is, or should be, one constant figure for class size is a myth.

Our public schools are already suffering from hardening of the arteries because they base many of their practices on inflexible concepts. In a world of exploding information and rapid change, fixed concepts of class size can only result in further roadblocks to progress. To prepare students to live in the future world, education must become increasingly personalized. A static figure for class size in such a world is a paradox. Since people are unique and their goals and capacities so varied, *no* ratio of teachers to pupils will *ever* be found to fit. Trying to find such a figure is impossible.

Asked how long he thought a man's legs ought to be, Abe Lincoln is reported to have said, "Long enough to reach from his body to the ground." Just so, the proper size for a class in a public school is the size required to get the job done. Some matters can best be dealt with in groups of thousands. For example, giving students the opportunity to watch an assembly of the United Nations on TV. Other learning opportunities may be better suited to much smaller groups, even groups of one. The size of the class also depends on the particular teacher and his or her most effective way of working. A tremendously effective lecturer's talents are wasted if he or she is assigned to work exclusively in small groups or laboratory settings. Conversely, the talented counselor or small group leader may be wasted when required to operate in large-group sessions or lecture halls.

How many students a teacher ought to work with is dependent on at least the following factors: (1) the subject matter being confronted, (2) the setting where the teaching takes place, (3) the needs and readiness of the students, (4) the equipment and supplies available, (5) the teacher's talents and abilities, and (6) the goals and purposes of the students and the teacher at a given time. Because so many of these factors are variable, a static figure for class size can only result in gross inefficiency. Far more important, frozen concepts of class size fail to meet the needs of thousands of students forced into learning molds that do not meet their needs, capacities, or current conditions.

An educational system designed to meet the changing needs of society on the one hand and the widely varying needs of youth on the other cannot afford to be stuck with the myth of constant class size. How schools are run and how classes are arranged must provide the widest possible flexibility so that teachers' talents, students' needs and abilities, and local resources can flow together in a constantly changing mix. If education is to dig itself out of its current morass and truly prepare students for the world they will live in, it will have to give up the grade level and class size myths. Thousands of modern teachers are already doing it. Experiments with ungraded primary schools, multi-age grouping, using older children to teach younger ones, learning centers, open classrooms, and many other innovations are slowly undermining the stranglehold these myths have had upon educational processes for generations.

NOTES

1. A. A. Sandin, *Social and Emotional Adjustment of Regularly Promoted and Non-Promoted Pupils* (New York: Bureau of Publications, Teachers College, Columbia University, 1944).

2. H. A. Caswell and A. W. Foshay, *Education in the Elementary School* (New York: American Book Company, 1950).

SELECTED READINGS

Blommers, P., and Coffield, W. "Effects of Non-promotion on Educational Achievement in the Elementary School." *Journal of Educational Psychology* 46 (1956): 237–49.

Finn, J. D. et al. "Teacher Expectations and Pupil Achievement: A Naturalistic Study." *Urban Education* 10 (1975): 175–97.

Schreiber, D., ed. *Profile of the School Dropout*. New York: Random House, Inc., 1967.

Silberman, C. *Crisis in the Classroom*. New York: Random House, Inc., 1970.

Walberg, H. J. et al. "Grade Level, Cognition and Affect: A Cross Section of Classroom Perceptions." *Journal of Educational Psychology* 64 (1973): 142–46.

Myths About
Teacher Responsibility

One of the unhappy side effects of attempting to reform education is the increased pressure placed upon teachers.[1] Sooner or later, all criticisms of the educational system end at their door. The demands we are currently making on teachers are bewildering beyond belief. Hundreds of innovations are being loudly pressed by educators, administrators, parents, industry, and government. The problems of civil rights, desegregation, tightening budgets, and rising or falling numbers of kids combined with these expectations for change make the teachers' tasks overwhelming. Add to this burden the continuous barrage of criticism teachers get from all sides and it is no wonder that many become dispirited and go about their tasks doggedly, plugging through one day after another, or drop out of the profession at the earliest opportunity.

Teachers are blamed for almost every imaginable failure of the educational system. Often this condemnation is totally undeserved. Because teachers stand at the place where "the buck stops," they are stuck with the inevitable outcomes of community failures to support schools adequately, inept school management, inflexible customs and traditions, out of date curricula, and many more. Especially, they are held responsible for the behavior of students, in school and out. No one would argue that teachers should not be accountable. But holding them responsible unjustly is not only unfair, it destroys morale and belittles their accomplishments. Even worse, it diverts attention from pressing educational problems badly in need of investigation and reform.

RESPONSIBILITY FOR STUDENT BEHAVIOR

Can teachers truly be held responsible for the behavior of their students? To answer that question we need to answer a prior one, namely: To what extent can *any* person, teacher or not, be held accountable for another person's behavior? Since behavior is never the exclusive product of any stimulus or set of stimuli provided by another person, it follows that no human being can ever be held responsible for the behavior of another except, perhaps, under three possible conditions: (1) when the other person is too weak or too sick to be responsible for himself or herself, (2) when one person makes another person dependent upon him or her, or (3) when responsibility is demanded by role definition.

When the Other Person Is Too Weak or Too Sick To Be Responsible

Grownups have to be responsible for some aspects of children's behavior, especially acts that might prove harmful to the child or to others. This same rule applies to persons too sick to be able to care for themselves. Acceptance of the responsibility to aid such persons has long been a basic tenet of Judeo-Christian philosophy. Such conditions of responsibility are comparatively short-lived, however, existing only until the individual can care for himself or herself. Generally speaking, the older children get, the more they must assume responsibility for themselves. This principle is clearly recognized in the courts. It is also the goal of human development as the human organism strives for freedom, autonomy, and self-actualization. It ought to be the goal of education as well.

When One Person Makes Another
Person Dependent

When one person takes upon himself or herself the responsibility for making decisions for another, that person has also assumed responsibility for the other's behavior. When a person has, for whatever reason, induced or seduced another to surrender his or her autonomy, that person has by so doing assumed responsibility for the other's actions. This may occur in the case of the physician who accepts the principle of total responsibility for the patient. It may also occur in the case of the psychotherapist who permits his or her client to develop a deep transference or in the case of a teacher who assumes the role of a child's mother. Such dependent relationships may sometimes be desirable in the doctor-patient relationship. In most of the other helping professions, which are not dependent on the helper *doing something to* his or her client, the development of such dependency is generally regarded as unfortunate and undesirable. Most modern approaches to psychotherapy, for example, carefully eschew the development of dependent relationships because strong dependence of the client on the therapist saps the client's own capacities to solve his or her problems and unduly prolongs the therapeutic relationship. Certainly the development of dependency can have little place in education, an institution whose basic objective is the production of intelligent persons who are capable of acting autonomously and freely with full responsibility for themselves.

When Responsibility Is Demanded
by Role Definition

Sometimes responsibility for another may be imposed on a person by virtue of his or her peculiarly assigned role. An example might be the responsibility of the prison guard to make certain that prisoners do not escape. Such role-defined responsibilities for the behavior of others, however, are usually extremely limited and generally restricted to preventive kinds of activities. So a teacher, by reason of role, might be held responsible for keeping two children from fighting with one another in the classroom. But holding the teacher responsible for whether or not a child does his or her homework is quite another question. Few of us have much direct control over even the simplest behaviors of other persons.

The basic democratic philosophy on which our society rests is "when people are free they can find their own best ways." Citizens are regarded as free and responsible agents. Each is held accountable for his or her own behavior, but very rarely for the behavior of others. Educators share these common responsibilities.

PROFESSIONAL RESPONSIBILITY

What of professional responsibility? For what can teachers be held accountable because they are teachers? Surely not for the behavior of students five years from now; too many others have had their fingers in that pie. A teacher's influence on all but the simplest, most primitive forms of student behavior, even in that teacher's own classroom, cannot be clearly established. The older children get, the less teachers can influence even those few, primitive forms of behavior. The attempt to hold teachers responsible for what students do is, for all practical purposes, well nigh impossible.

We are accustomed to thinking of the proper model for teaching in terms of the medical model—the doctor who knows, telling the patient who doesn't, what the problem is and what must be done. Such an approach to human beings works fine when dealing with their bodies; their bodies can be manipulated by some outside force. Applied to teaching, this model produces a concept of teachers as makers, forcers, molders, or coercers of learning. When dealing with the growth and development of human personalities, the reverse of the medical model is more often required. When changes to be produced must be made inside the individual, where they cannot be directly manipulated, it is the student who knows and the teacher who does not. Such shifts in our thinking make the act of teaching a process of ministering to student growth rather than a process of control and management of behavior. Teachers are asked to be facilitators rather than controllers, helpers rather than directors. They are asked to be assisters, encouragers, enrichers, inspirers.

Teachers can and should be held accountable for behaving professionally. What distinguishes a profession from more mechanical occupations is its dependence upon the worker as a thinking, problem-solving being.[2] The effective professional worker is one who has learned how to use himself or herself, how to use his or her knowledge and skills effectively and efficiently to carry out individual and society's purposes. Professional teachers, therefore, can properly be held accountable for at least four things:

1. Teachers can be held accountable for being informed in subject matter. This is so self-evident, it needs no further discussion.
2. Teachers can be held responsible for being concerned about the welfare of students and knowledgeable about their behavior. Professional educators need the most accurate and sensitive understandings about children and their behavior possible. This also seems self-evident, but it is all too often violated in practice. The beliefs many teachers hold about what students are like and why they behave as they do are sometimes little short of mythology. False and inadequate concepts abound throughout the profession and find expression in practices that are not only hindering but often downright destructive.

3. Teachers can be held responsible for the purposes they seek to carry out. Human behavior is purposive. Each teacher behaves in terms of what he or she believes is the purpose of society, of society's institutions, of the schoolroom, of learning a subject, of interacting with students, and, most especially, of his or her own personal needs and goals. The purposes held by educators provide the basic dynamics from which practices are evolved. They are the fundamental causes of teacher and administrator behavior and determine the nature of what goes on in classrooms and the schools and systems in which they exist. As a consequence, if education is to achieve its fundamental objectives, any plan of accountability must give the exploration of educators' purposes an important place.

4. Teachers can be held responsible for the methods they use to carry out their own and society's purposes. This does not mean that educators must utilize some previously determined "right" methods. So far as anyone can determine, there are no such things. Professional responsibility does not demand a prescribed way of behaving. What it does require is that the methods used have the presumption of being good for the client. The emphasis is not on guaranteed outcomes, but on the defensible character of what is done. Doctors, for example, are not held responsible for the death of the patient. What they are held responsible for is that what they did had the presumption of being helpful in the eyes of their peers. Teachers, too, must be prepared to stand this kind of professional scrutiny. Whatever they do should be for some good and sufficient reason, defensible in terms of rational thought, experience, or as a consequence of informal or empirical research.

In the research on good and poor teachers done at the University of Florida, good teachers stood up very well under the four criteria mentioned.[3] Good teachers seem to have developed, in the course of their growth and experience, positive perceptions of their subject matter, themselves, children, purposes, and methods. This happened without anyone consciously attempting to instill them. One wonders what might be done to improve the quality of teaching by a systematic process of helping teachers explore and discover more adequate conceptions in each of these areas.

In the preoccupation with behavioral objectives and performance-based criteria approaches to accountability, the four factors involved in professional competence mentioned here have been given little attention. If we could be assured of high levels of professional responsibility in school personnel, many of the problems of accountability would solve themselves. Speaking as a parent, I would be quite content to entrust the education of my children to professionally responsible teachers who understood behavior, were concerned about kids, knew their subjects, ascribed to positive purposes, and were willing and able to discuss and defend the practices they engaged in. If I had that, I would feel little need to assess their productivity. I could rest content that in the process of responsibly carrying out their own professional goals, they were also contributing to mine, my children's, and society's.

NOTES

1. Much of the material in this chapter is adapted from A. W. Combs, *Educational Accountability: Beyond Behavior Objectives* (Washington, D.C.: Association for Supervision and Curriculum Development, 1972).

2. A. W. Combs, R. A. Blume, A. J. Newman and H. L. Wass, *The Professional Education of Teachers: The Education of Teachers* (Boston: Allyn and Bacon, Inc., 1974).

3. A. W. Combs, ed., *Florida Studies in the Helping Professions*, University of Florida Monographs in the Social Sciences, No. 37 (Gainesville, Florida: University of Florida Press, 1969).

SELECTED READINGS

Frymeir, J. R. "Professionalism in Context." *Ohio State Law Journal* 26 (1965): 53–64.

Goodlad, J. I. "Perspective on Accountability." *Phi Delta Kappan* 57 (1975): 108–12.

Stinnett, T. M., and Hugett, A. J. "The Profession of Teaching." *Professional Problems of Teachers.* New York: Macmillan, Inc., 1966.

Epilogue

The myths discussed in this book are only a few of the many that impede innovation and change in education. They were selected because they are of special interest to me. A brief look at any school system will quickly reveal many other myths that contribute to the frustration of students and teachers and obstruct satisfying achievement of our educational goals. The following are additional myths suggested by teachers' groups with whom I have worked:

- Today's youth are inferior to those of a generation ago
- Mind is separate from body and should be separately trained
- Knowledge exists outside the learner
- The young are naturally opposed to learning
- Uniqueness is evil; conformity is good
- Standards are what *we* establish for *them*
- Someone always must win and someone lose
- Test results are infallible
- Teachers don't really care
- Morality can only be taught by religion
- Schools teach the truth

- Compulsory attendance is an absolute necessity
- People learn best from repetition
- Good students are the quiet ones; problem students are the noisy and disruptive ones
- There is no place for anger in schools—on the part of teachers or students
- Schools must avoid dealing with controversial matters
- People need to learn to accept what is
- Good citizens always obey
- An educated person is more worthwhile than an uneducated one
- Masculinity means strong, aggressive, nonemotional
- Femininity means soft, yielding, compliant
- It's good for people to learn to fit in
- People are worthwhile only on the basis of what they do
- Getting back to the basics will save us
- Teachers are never quite good enough
- Idleness is bad
- Distasteful matters like anger, fear, hate, greed and dishonesty are topics to be avoided in school
- Anybody can be something and probably should
- Because things can be taught much earlier, they should be
- Our country—right or wrong

No doubt you will have your own favorites to add to the list. So much the better. Bringing our myths to light is the first essential step in doing something about them. To persist in the grip of our myths will make it impossible to meet the challenge of our changing world. To solve the problems of modern education we need to base our thinking on the most accurate beliefs we can find. We cannot afford to become the prisoners of our own misperceptions. Our youth deserve much better.